DEEPER WATERFALLS

LILLIE JOHNSON

authorHOUSE®

AuthorHouse™
1663 Liberty Drive
Bloomington, IN 47403
www.authorhouse.com
Phone: 833-262-8899

This is a work of fiction. All of the characters, names, incidents, organizations, and dialogue in this novel are either the products of the author's imagination or are used fictitiously.

Published by AuthorHouse 08/14/2020

ISBN: 978-1-7283-7042-2 (sc)
ISBN: 978-1-7283-7095-8 (e)

Print information available on the last page.

Any people depicted in stock imagery provided by Getty Images are models, and such images are being used for illustrative purposes only.
Certain stock imagery © Getty Images.

This book is printed on acid-free paper.

Scripture quotations marked KJV are from the Holy Bible, King James Version (Authorized Version). First published in 1611. Quoted from the KJV Classic Reference Bible, Copyright © 1983 by The Zondervan Corporation.

CONTENTS

PREFACE

I give thanks to almighty Yahweh, who has blessed me with this beautiful gift, and I pray Yahweh blesses every soul who reads this book. Without him, my books would not be possible as I can't put two sticks together. He has blessed me with beautiful words through dreams, visions, and thoughts, and I give Him all the praises. Yahweh has been too good to humankind; the world's tears should cause a bigger flood than the first because looking at the true picture from our unselfish hearts, we'd see that Yeshua died for all! Knowing our evil selves and with Yahweh becoming the sacrificial Lamb for us, how can we go on with evil living in our hearts When he was and is the greatest love of all? When He kicked Satan from heaven and the angels, He could have destroyed them, but He did not.

In the garden of Eden, He could have made another Eve, but He knew nothing would change. Like Satan, Eve and Adam were given free will. A world free of darkness, but it is not this one. Satan was perfect. So were Adam and Eve until they allowed disobedience and an itching curiosity to enter their hearts.

Hate, evil, racism, and all forms of darkness won't be allowed in the New Jerusalem, so let's repent, fast, and continually pray, and not let go of Yahweh's hand. Let's embrace and endure life because it will be worth it, worth it in the new heaven and earth that was intended. Please don't fall asleep. "Therefore keep watch, because you do not know on what day Yeshua will come" (Matt. 24:42).

A LILY IN THE DESERT

Happy Mother's Day

Not knowing the pain or the number of tears a mother cries for her child,
Not knowing the pain or the number of tears a mother cries for her child.
Only knowing the love she gives me,
Unconditional, undying love.
When you see a flower, you see only its beauty.
You do not see the area in which it has grown.
A desert boils by day and freezes by night,
And yet a beautiful flower has grown.
Weeds and thorns rip up from the ground only to destroy.
Storms come and go, winds rush and blow,
but Yah never lets you go.
My mother never let her storms overcome her.
I stand in awe for I was birthed by an angel.

—Seanna Lackey

A MAN AND HIS CONSCIENCE

I have no meaning; my cursed skin of black the lowest of names, I am called "nigger."
Lied to all my life, worked hard, nothing to hold except my finger on the trigger.
The children I raised for eighteen years, DNA says today are not mine but another man's genetics.
Years of my wife's belittling, looking in the mirror, I was a man then; now I am nothing, broken down and pathetic.
I gave her everything she wanted; her smile and charm were not real—100 percent synthetic.
"I love you," came from her tender lips like a beautiful waterfall.
I never abused her or the children; I was always there at her beckoning call,
Standing beside her always, uplifting her for being herself, great and never small.
When we walked into a room, it was she who made me feel brave and tall.
What happened? We were happy ... I want to end my life and into the grave crawl.
Misunderstandings? There were not any. Questions? I am beating my head against the wall.
Love was all I had to give—along with our children, the house, cars, her enormous wardrobe.
Whatever she wanted I did and gave, whether here in America or around the globe.
I worked so extremely hard, and sometimes I wanted to quit. I could not—I am a man.
The doctors say I have terminal cancer, and she lets go of my hand.
Picking up falling crumbs, I try to make sense of it all and still do not understand.
Maybe she is grieving; I do not know. Dying was not my plan.
If the tables were turned, I would not leave; by her side I would continue to stand.

A messenger delivered divorce papers to me signed six months ago with a note she is marrying another man.

Six months? I am going crazy in my mind.

We were always together; how and when did another relationship she find?

Work was the only time we were apart. Pathetic, I am, stupid and blind.

The children and she were my sun that always shined.

Holding these papers, hurt, angry, confused, what is left but my missing signature on the bottom line?

Handed these papers in the hospital today; why should I bother?

These papers showing me instead of keeping it hidden till I am gone this hurtful truth.

Divorce papers with her arrogance … proof!

It is crazy; I was a good man even with her abuse, a loving husband and father.

Never questioned the children's paternity, even though they did not look like me.

I love them; I focus on our home and making us happy.

Whatever she asked of me I sincerely gave. What a shame; I have loaded the gun.

The dreams, memories on the beach building sandcastles under the evening sun.

Kids filling their pails, laughing, playing, having fun.

Under the moonlight into the waters we had run.

Thinking now, I should have asked, Was I the one?

I did right by my family. Six months or longer divorce she contemplated?

No, Abigail, you were my heart and soul; you, Delilah, have castrated.

No remorse, no nothing; you stand proudly after my heart you serrated!

How long these hurtful lies have you orchestrated?

"I do not love you," came from her mouth, along with my presence she hated.

This family path we traveled was deceptive, twisted, crooked, and never straight.

Her inconspicuous role or desiring marriage and all her forbidden fruits I ate.

Not having my family there is no hope, happiness, or fight left in me … it is too late.

Coming into this once beautiful world alone, I depart alone through death's peaceful gates.

Her leaving me and not seeing our children again, gun in my hand, I refuse to wait.

Hurt stares me in the face and truth's spoon blended with suicide' I eat from its detonated plate.

Seeing her naked body in the past, today evil were the seeds her soul impregnated.

Terminal cancer is too slow; bullets in the gun, nothing to debate.

It is what it is ... truth she did not love me, and death is my escape,

Life's cruel reality handed to me from my destined fate.

A MOTHER'S CAUTIONS

❖

To see her walking down a broken road,
Praying Yah to give her strength to carry life's unpredictable loads,
Your biggest fear, you realize, was not her falling and scrapping her knee.
Losing herself within a world of hate, hidden between the leaves of destiny,
Trying to fit in with the crowd so desperately.
Hope she does not forget her happiness; she holds the key.
Not to change herself, trying on many façades that others want her to be.
In the forest, losing herself hiding behind the trees.
Her mother's caution signs, but no longer she sees,
Blinded by what she thinks she needs.
He is not the one, a mother prays to the Father above.
She lets go, taking off the coverings of her heart and her once-fitting glove,
Constantly chasing the idea of what she thought was love.
Loving him the way she does, letting go is not simple, like a sneeze or cough.
Falling into depression every night, teary mask of make-believe happiness she takes off,
Trying to hide the sadness her mother already sees.
Ignoring her mother, between the lines she refused to read.
Daily his licks, lies, and, "I am sorry," were growing seeds.
Running to him, like a pig at a trough; is it time to feed?
A mother's prayers, a mother's cautions; it is time I get out this ring and take the lead!
His lies, my heart, I thought were all I would ever need.
She held her caution signs up, and yet I did not take heed.
Years have flown; lust has come and gone.
My head in my mother's lap in my room at home.
His spell I am not under, the feelings no stronger.
Mother, I understand it is not so bad being alone.
I am sorry for thinking you were controlling. I was wrong.
Thank you again for your patience and kindness.

Realizing now my mother's caution signs and many prayers she would pray
Are beautiful, not harsh words she would say.
And I am reminded of her undying love that never faded away!

—Seanna Lackey

AND THEN YOU DIE

⚜

What are you seeking in this life—
House on a hill, kids, partner, or homemaker wife?
What you seek, is it something you are focused on, no matter if your heart
Is determined and willing?
The biggest mansion, expensive cars, the best of everything, the world-famous
Architect, the tallest building? Or
Be simple and content with whatever you are blessed to get?
Your dreams and goals you want to conquer; first you must plan and set.
"I want to feed the hungry all around the world,"
Says the little one who looks at his mom with no food to eat.
Their days are of nothing, are bright and sunny even when the clouds are dim.
He gets a molded piece of bread from his pocket, and they give thanks.
"And a little child shall lead them."
Others would not see this reality as hope, but dark and grim.
Whether you are gathering wood for the fire or morsels of food and scrap,
You are comfortable at your mountains of fortune; it does not mean you are exempt from life's mishaps.
Your mighty pride says poverty are "those" people's preordained trap;
My wealth and their bearings will never be on the same page or map.
I had to work for my earnings; I was not lazy or on welfare, I worked hard
And took a lot of crap!
There were not any handouts for me; I worked, not like a useless pimp.
Fortune, fame, and wealth, on this list I am no longer exempt!
In a class all by myself,
I enjoy the finest foods, buy the most expensive art, go places only in one's imagination.
I stand alone at the mountaintop, desiring nothing.
My mornings, nights, and times on the clock hands I need not watch; I am Father Time.

Hard work, work hard, was my subliminal message in the core of my wanting heart and mind.

At the top, my accomplishments are like the sun that shines.

All will gaze upon me; I alone endured and am worthy to stand at the front of the line,

Not feeling conscience-stricken for the ones left behind.

No welfare given, no commodities, enduring and embracing disastrous necessities, up the mountain

I climbed.

In life, hard work pays, not like a silver dollar you undeservedly find.

I am the farmer who planted the seeds and cultivated the crops' fields and vines.

I will enjoy its vegetables and fruits in their proper seasons and time.

Hard work repeated, pouring the water, the handle to the pump I primed.

No, life was not easy, loving, or kind.

Broken plans, dreams, but I succeeded; grains and crumbs, but I made it by myself.

Persistent were the seeds I planted, and my paradise has flourished like a beautiful flower.

I have it all: money, fame, wealth, power!

Yah said, "Unknowingly that was his last breath,

No matter your accomplishments, in the end low or high,

and then you die."

APPLES, COCONUT YOGURT, AND ALMOND MILK

❖

I cannot imagine my life without you; my heart gives praises to Yah
because you held my hand in clouds of white and times of hurting blue.
I do not know many things, but your existence's laugh and the life you
continue
to bring into my heart of many saddened tears. Knowing I am loved by you
breaks my fearful ring.
Warm bath, candles, and peaceful music the birds sing.
I know Yahweh is the Creator of all things ... life; into mine you are
placed.
My tears of never being alone within its shadow I stand. I am here at
home, and
you are there. I feel you and your love holding my aching heart and
wrinkled hands.
How can this once tiny being grow up to be my training wheels? And
myself, Stacey,
Understands. I sit here writing a note with pen in my hand. "It's Love"
is not so much big or gigantic things or roses, lilies, or the finest silk.
Warm bath, apples, coconut yogurt, and almond milk.
I knew you were precious when I birthed you into this hurting
world. Looking at you, I see my mom, who has passed on. But her spirit
from Yah
In your eyes roams.
I know and continue to pray in the New Jerusalem we will dwell in our
home.
Memories of holding your hand when you were a little girl, now grown.
And the light that was in her I still see in you, my loving daughter. I know
it was not the
world that hurt us ... but life, on its path, Yah's light now shines bright.
The storms, depression, and darkness with the Father make those times
of struggles
and trying to find ourselves in the present day okay, all right.

With His Spirit we can conquer all oncoming fights!

Our bond of love will forever be in this momentary life. I

no longer feel all the hurt from my mom's passing in 1984.

It is all gone—hurt, guilt, shame; because of you, I closed that door.

It goes back to a warm bath, apples, coconut yogurt, and almond milk. The love deeper

and smoother than the world's finest silk. Thanking Yah for you my hands and heart to

Him I lift. For this tiny being, my training wheels, my loving, and much-needed gift.

Dabs of perfume my mom used to wear on a towel I sniff.

If I were a door, I would want you to be my knob's handle.

Relaxing in a warm bath surrounded by sweet burning candles.

My loving daughter.

A TREE

If trees could talk, would man listen or try to claim?
Would he put us in a lab, clone, dissect, or devein?
Into his experimental lab, trees like monkeys would he train?
Our existence in his mind try to explain.
His mind is like a library of unread books.
The gift YHWH made us, we are caught on the end of his evil hooks.
We used to be beautiful; our leaves and worth his machines shook.
Once-sweet clean waters we drank from are now contaminated brooks.
Into the mirrors of hope are no more, and death is our future; our beauty he took.
Our branches, roots, and bark is engraved his name?
He thinks he is YHWH; ungrateful self should repent and be ashamed.
Would he open his heart, our tears and the root of our dying branches take the blame?
Would he try to inhale the oxygen that YHWH gave us and put in a bottle?
When our branches are weak, will our roots he tends to like a loving sitter?
When he has polluted the heavens, auction the souls of my family, and sells to the highest bidder,
Would he be loving and listen to their cries and leave them be?
His evildoings have been in the making for countless ages.
Nothing happens overnight but in planned stages.
His work, his DNA, tries to duplicate, and his fraudulent works lie between scientific pages.
The animals know what man has done, and wonder why the heavens thunder and the ocean rages.
Man, greedy self, captures them and puts in cages.
I am a tree, and YHWH put us here for a reason; man has penetrated the ozone and put everything off balance.
The oceans and seas, rivers, brooks, and all the waters between.
The earth has been crying for many years; he keeps building and polluting.
The food is not worth eating; the human body is eating its own death.

Chemical plants have polluted the air; the wind blows its poisonous gases everywhere.

His heart is gone, and love and hope no longer abide there.

His evil works are the fruits he bears.

The earth is dying, and man is the reason; he will be judged by YHWH.

He thinks he can rule the world and all life.

He did not give me mine, but he is taking it away with every fallen tree.

The waters were blue and clear, the air was fresh, and the winds were harmless.

Oil and filth pour into the blackened blue; we drink from it, and YHWH cries.

Man, he cannot hear because he does not care anymore.

Its healings man kept for himself;

Plants, herbs, things from the earth are medicine that YHWH gave.

One day soon the world will be one gigantic grave.

So much for his library of unread books; evil is the road he wickedly paved.

My once-clothed limbs and bark he has shaved.

His mind is more dangerous than any untamed beast.

Picture a world without him, and you would have a *masterpiece*.

Man's name should have been abortion; unknown sounds better.

His formulas and documents are written on my dead parts transformed into a letter.

The seasons were set for their months man without his calendar would not know.

His man-made crossbreeding life in the waters; I cry because he is evil!

The trees, seas, birds, and bees obey the Father, not wanting to be the Creator.

We could not be; we are living things without a soul, knowing YHWH made the rocks, seaweed, and sand.

In his library of unread books, like a king he stands.

He wants to control everything, his doing, death he holds in his wicked hands.

Experimenting on life, the world was formed and void, a dying world is his plan?

Life was given to all by YHWH, heavens deep, all creatures, the entire land.

He has made himself god; filled with wickedness, he refuses to understand.

I am a dying tree, and I wish Yahweh never made man!

BEDPANS

Question asked, What do you want to do or be when you grow up, little girls and boys?
I would like to be the coach for the Chicago Bears in Illinois.
For orphans around the world, I want to have a factory filled with free toys.
I want to be a firefighter, I want to be a doctor, I want to be the quarterback for the Dallas Cowboys.
A fan at WrestleMania cheering for the good guys making noise.
I want to bake my grandma's delicious lemon pies for the county fair.
I pray, God not let children be abused anymore, hoping He answers my prayer.
I want God to make the lame walk and throw away all the wheelchairs.
I want to be a pastor, spreading the word of truth everywhere.
I want to be a freedom leader, for the walls of injustices for all people to no longer be here or there.
I want to be a schoolteacher, a lawyer, a janitor, a computer technician.
Drums, piano, I want to be a famous musician.
My hands are blessed; my dream is to be a multiracial beautician.
I want to be like my uncle; he is a mortician.
I want to join the circus and be a magician.
Little minds filled with seeds of hope and ambitions.
Old sayings be careful of life's overflowing deadly, unpredictable fountains.
Life has many stairways, delays, pitfalls, and slippery mountains.
The devil with his temptations, crumbs leading to a trail of heartache, sits back and laughs.
Growing up in this fast-paced world, meeting your better-half.
So in love with this unknown person, in your naïve heart, plans of a happy life.
Telling Mom and Dad, he/she is the one, no need to think twice.
Your soul mate, girlfriend, boyfriend planned a wedding, becoming husband and wife.
A year of marriage, and everything has changed.
Couch, table, and chairs are not the only things that have been rearranged.

I thought the house we purchased was vinyl, not brick. That is strange.

Looking at him/her, they still look the same.

Remembering a week ago in the kitchen, I swear he/she called me someone's else's name.

Planned a party, invited all these people from the job; into our house they came.

I am not sure about any of this, but he/she said I agreed to it, now him/her I blamed.

I do not know anymore; working all the time, I do not have time for silly games.

I am the easy one; whatever you throw, I catch.

A year of this is tiresome; I no longer want to fetch.

Not the same person who held my hand at the mall, eating a burger, from my milkshake taking a sip.

Saying you love me, now I cannot believe it is coming out of the same mouth and tender kissing lips.

The other week calling me that name; was it an honest slip?

I love you with all my hurting heart, I forgave you too many times in this unloving marriage.

I thought my love would be enough, that I could continue to nurture like a baby in a carriage.

You never loved me; when I said, "I do," I was taking on all your unknown baggage!

I had several promotions, starting with the standard bed pan.

The tiny things you did I pushed away with my hand.

Life did not get better; your garage of pans increased, from the fractured to the Polar Ware

Stainless steel pan.

I accepted all your crap, being the autoclavable, whatever comfortable pan you needed.

Loving me I did not; today, getting up, I understand.

Movies, milkshakes, roller skating—you had a plan.

Letting go of this—you—my heart your feet will no longer stand!

Take, no, keep your lies and deceiving smile.

Bariatric and all other pans staked in a pile.

Your sweet words, charm, and touch are vile.

Pretty ain't the picture.

Your batter is deceit's selfishness; sugarless lies in the mixture.

Questions answered, no one knows what path leads up the road.

Few accept the truth and continue to remain in a loveless relationship, carrying someone's load.

We are blooming flowers, not other people's tools they use for a commode! Answered.

You are more delectable than preserves in a Mason jar.

You are a person with a tender heart, not a remote-controlled car.

Boys and girls, grow up to be what you are destined to be—a diamond of a star!

BLACK

❖

A beautiful woman with her blonde wavy hair, rounded lips, and a nice figure,
Stands in her office, looking out the window of one of the biggest law firms.
Having everything she ever wanted, says within her heart, I had to work harder
Then any man because I would not accept their terms.
When conversating with me, working between the sheets was their only concern.
Worse than a pack of wolves, picture-proof waste less sperm!
I worked like no other person, nothing handed, everything earned.
I am here—over barrels, hurdles, man-made mountains and dead ends—ignoring
Repeated sexual remarks, along with, "This job requires balls."
I prayed, cried, crawled, and continued up man's corporate ladder.
I did it my way—clean, honest, hiding behind no one's shadow.
These racist pigs and their ignorant remarks, not letting others in because
Their skin is either red, yellow, brown, or dark.
Being told you are lucky to be here, just go along; bunch of bullies like dogs, no bite but bark.
The shit I endured, kicked, pulled, and cut in pieces mending myself together.
Making it to the top is all that mattered.
You are too cute for this, you are in the wrong business—caveman mentality.
I was not flattered.
Countless times my work others were credited with; I pressed on, praise was not
my destination.
Multiple times in their eyes compared to glass, I was too thick; I refused
To be shattered!
The only one in this position, their looks and senseless speeches, having to
Clean up their shit like I was the maid.

Long hours, overworked, few breaks, underpaid.
Behind closed doors, their numbers so many in the trash, wanting to get laid.
Determination runs through my veins; of their intimidation, I was not afraid.
Letting their lower body parts speak, a ridiculous trade.
"I wash your back, you wash mine." All that shit I poured down the drain like lemonade.
Sleeping with these serpents is not the road I am willing to pave.
At their "manly meetings" could not speak; my solutions they stole while throwing
Dirt on me, trying to bury me in an unknown grave.
The more they took from me, the more I gave.
Looking out the windows, I begin to cry. I am a white woman; in their eyes no better
Than a slave.
I made it not by my looks but my intellectual mind.
For a moment I went back to a place I almost forgot in time.
Unlocking a desk drawer, with a picture my mom gave me on her dying bed,
Afraid of the afterlife's unmentioned truths she said.
These two people, one my mom, this man being told today my dad.
I refuse to accept; her weakening voice, crying apologies, should-haves in another time.
In another life, this man she was in love with, she knew had a wife.
Today these truths hurt deeper than a French knife.
How could she be so selfish and hide the truth?
Tears falling from my heart like rain from a tin roof.
Facing death, lying on its bed, telling me life events, and handing me proof.
I could not believe but accepted, a lifetime being told in an hour.
Holding my arm, I wipe the tears from my mother's eyes.
I am bending over, wondering if there are more hidden lies.
Her throat is dry and thirsty; a cup of water to her mouth she tiredly sips.
Her fragile body and wrinkled hands and arms, like many roads being traveled,
Asks for forgiveness from her desert lips.

Frightened, before my eyes my mother is dying. I look at her IV bags; morphine
mildly drips.
I feel strange as a breath of coldness brushes against my hips.
Tears from her eyes, she lets go of my arm; the pain is so intense, the PCA button
She presses repeatedly and grips.
I am praying she will be able to tell all before out of this life she slips.
I am worried, angry, confused, hurting, and saddened at the same time.
"Mother," I ask softly, "How could you be so unkind?"
"Baby," she said, "you do not understand. What I did was wrong. All these years
Being tortured in my mind.
I knew what I did, and like so many others, I turned deaf ears, and the truth became blind."
I was wrestling with my conscience; I could not let my mother leave this world and forgiveness
From me she did not find.
She said she was sorry, not giving me a sister or brother.
I was the outcome of the love they shared with each other.
"For my biggest sin, terminal cancer is my justly portion.
I love your father, and I could not go through with a horrible abortion.
If I agreed, it would have ended holding a dying straw.
You and this picture are all I have of him. He died because of a lie, and during that
Time it was an unjust law.
This love triangle, knowing about her, complicated picture the brushes draw.
We had discussed many times what would happen, foolishly being captured
In life's murderous jigsaw.
We knew they would kill us in a blink and not hesitate.
It was a Wednesday; they pulled back the drapes.
Crosses burning, dogs barking in the distance, no means of escape.
He said, 'I love you, keep our child, see to her lips tasting the finest wine, the purest grapes.'
Rushing through the doors dogs, guns, torches. I yelled rape.

Beating him with ignorance, hatred, evil, its bat they repeatedly swung.
No judge, jury, that Wednesday your father was hung."
She held my hand tightly, asking again for forgiveness; I gave. "I love you," and
"I am so sorry," were her last words and breath.
Standing alone with heartbreaking truths and the presence of death.
Forgiveness she waited for, and shame, guilt, and all hurt on a Wednesday left.
Crying and smiling, looking at my dad's picture, I am not white.

BROKEN WORLD, BROKEN PEOPLE

We rise to do what we want, seeking the comfort of the mighty dollar.
We base everything on its value, like the muscles within our neck or the
Buttons that lead to one's shirt collar.
Submitting to our lusts and evil deeds are the paths we follow.
When hurt has its claws within, we raise our voice to YHWH and holla.
Blaming YHWH for our wickedness, taking drugs to numb self are the
pills we swallow.
We do not want the truth; looking in the mirror there is nothing to see,
no substance, value.
Greed and a lifeless soul that is hollow.
We are running every day from the truth, with its clouds of sorrow, shame,
and amnesia.
Temporarily we turn to the devil's bottle.
False hope … it gets me through all situations.
The chains of our foolish decisions daily are the outcome of our failing
foundation.
Not knowing if my heart is reprobate, shoes tied, and soul crossed.
My path leads to heaven, hell, or the grave; either way, I am lost!
The truth is over here—no, over there; like a wave you are unstable, being
tossed.
What, the chicken or egg, hen, or whatever came first?
It does not matter; I believe in science and Mother Universe.
I can do all things not believing in some YHWH by whom my ancestors
were cursed.
When it is over, it does not matter if I am thrown in the sea, coffin, or
driven hearse.
I look at the world and the making of man, so I unravel the stitches to my
fleshy purse.
I take out all that was embedded in my mind as a child.
Born into poverty, faith, and hope, seeing hate took away my smile.
The world and its wealth, sickness, death, lying prophets, preachers, when
Will they be put on trial?

Killer chemical plants, lying lawyers, greedy doctors, and their evil adds
to the pile.
Their dirty deeds and evils have been erased from life's file.
Angry little boy, now man, eat my words and you will understand.
Adam to Methuselah, Noah, Moses all had a plan.
Disobedience is what caused separation from YHWH to man.
Repent, my son, follow; take the cross, and hold onto my hand.
I will prepare a place, and wickedness will never dwell in the land.
Your house I entered, and darkness and greed were everywhere.
My child, look to me and not selfish man.
On My words you may fall, but My truth will forever stand.
But Father, I went to the church and prayed beneath its steeple.
My son, it is not a broken world, just broken people!

CHAINS

Chains and whips came with diseases and sickness, racism and whips; O freedom land, freedom land,
where have you gone?
Building a better world for you; centuries, centuries, I still do not belong.
Searching in an unknown land, worked like a mule, not allowed to have a home.
Our necks under their feet, our weakened backs, their whips forever strong.
Taken from our land of plenty, no chains, whips, into their land the winds have blown.
Our sweat and tears by their tortured whips have their fields of plenty grown.
What about us, chains and whips, boats and ships? You've seen our worth for your selfish, greedy Investors!
Thinking you took our souls, rape, torture, your justice laws given to a world of molesters.
Time has passed, but I still experience the burdens, the cries for freedom from the graves of my Ancestors.
What's changed?
Chains, chains, freedom, freedom, another time, different whips, your laws, our uncovered protection?
High on the hill, scrolling in our neighborhoods and congregations, telling lies. What time is it? Election!
Whips that sting, politicians the chains that cling taken from our necks, headed in the same direction.
O freedom land, freedom land, where have you gone?
The clouds have cleared; the declaration is here, yet we still live in fear.
Freedom for who?
You, you, and minorities, not you?
I still feel the whips' stings; I still hear the chains' cling. Bleeding from inside,
You will never understand the pain that dwells in our eyes.
You are the whips that continue to bruise and kick our sides.

New world order we know is about to rise!

Peace for the entire world … more lies!

Injustices, injustices

For minorities, not asked but thrown onto this hateful ride.

You have made yourself God; there are no limits to your whips, your chains, our unforeseen freedom,

Your mountains of pride.

Your continual victory, year or two later, what's changed? Nothing; you lied!

Chains, whips, Underground Railroad, Africa-Jerusalem, Lord Almighty, there is no place to hide.

Emeralds, rubies, gold, myrrh, rosemary, satin, silk we had! Descendants of one of the twelve tribes.

Chains, chains, invisible to the eyes, washed onto a land of slavery by hate's tide.

Some say the hands of our own took the bribe.

Whatever, truth be told, our freedom taken by greedy, selfish thieves.

Their evil has been covered by hate's falling leaves.

Over here, over there, people being raped by the priests, government, the entire system hidden amongst the trees.

Over there, over here, bunch of genocidal Pharisees!

Whips and chains, chains and whips.

The time is now to call Yahweh's name and break the chains!

All unrepented evildoers will enter hell's flames!

—Seanna Lackey

FAILED

What has not failed in this corrupt world? Man has not learned his lesson, and confusion insists on building

That tower.

We will never have justice and equality for all races, not in this day or future hours.

The ones who lied when running for office changed having tasted a little greed and power.

No change; the seeds had already been planted in their hearts, the only growth the petals of an

Uncaring flower.

Are we listening to their lying speeches, or are our minds covered by blackened wool?

Tingling, itching ears feel good moments; the truth not listening is string they will not pull.

A lie they accept within knowing its stench is the dung of a bull.

Eyes like the ocean, never full.

Cannot see the forest for the trees.

These people are liars they easily believe.

Singing a better world, better times waiting for tomorrow.

How so when these people are the ones circling in the skies, releasing poisons, creating man-made sorrows?

Indebted to other countries, doing things that ought not be, they continue to borrow.

No, it is not yours anymore; in time the people will be faced with unimaginable horrors.

You have robbed Peter to pay Paul.

Your debt is higher than the trees standing tall.

Didn't you know or care? One day the debtors your bill they are going to call.

Look in the mirror at shattered pieces of arrogance; you are not so big anymore but lied out and small.

Changes being made today have been planned before you came along; it is much deeper

Than the shutdown and higher than the wall.

You schedule an appointment for you and your crew; a jet you have chartered.

It is another meeting; thought you weren't seen on the beach in Key West, Florida?

Presidents Abraham, Nixon, Reagan, and Carter.

Seeds were being planted for New World Order!

When the truth hits the fire and this unjustly system has failed,

Those who are on Yahweh's side will be released from its bars of hate and no longer be jailed.

Then you will see your world system has failed.

That day you will not be bailed.

These truths have been written, my disciples shall tell

Matthew 16:18, upon this rock the gates of hell shall not prevail!

FALLING ROCKS

✦

Am I missing something standing on the mountain's top?
I worked hard to get where I am, still I am being framed, handcuffed by these prejudiced cops.
I labored in the fields, tending to someone's crops.
I did not ask for my ancestors' promised forty acres or mule, just my props.
Worked twice as hard to get here, being treated like a janitor who sweeps the floor and then mops.
Present time, I feel someone has turned back the hands on the clock.
I did my time in the valley, still being hit, moving around; I am a man, not a rabbit hiding in the hole he hops.
The only way to get through is embrace each hit as they drop.
As the world turns, it's déjà vu, nothing changing; these happenings are not going to stop.
This is life, whether I like it or not, I do understand.
In their eyesight in this race, having won all the medals, I am still not characterized as a man.
That is okay because I know who I am, from the sweat on my back and the calluses on feet and hands.
Mankind? I am thankful for blessings, curses, and the hard rains from above.
Whatever man throws at me—hate, wickedness—I will catch in my spiritual glove.
The anger that grew in my heart, I exchanged it with YHWH's love.
In the past I was like the southern cassowary, today a gentle dove.
I let go of the misguided things in the past that my heart could not breathe, being smothered.
I am a child of the King and blessed to be protected with His covering.
I look beyond mankind's outer layers and his sinful hovering.
I am thankful I did not let the things I've accomplished go to my heart, losing my sanity.
Along the path I followed, knowing and not knowing its end, vanity.
Once again, I know who I am and to whom I belong.

History cannot be changed; it happened. Today we do what we do, and tomorrow we will be judged right or wrong.

If injustice hits you daily, whatever race you are, this here is our temporarily home.

People wanting heaven on earth, not accepting YHWH. Hand in Satan's cookie jars, searching for

something you continue to roam.

Needle in your arm—does not matter what drug—break the rocks that is being thrown!

Young girl on the corner, now old woman, you are not alone.

Kid at school being bullied, too afraid to tell, cries at night, overdoses, his abusers are here.

He is gone.

Mother cannot feed her kids; thinking they will be better off, calls 911 and blows her brains out, cries the operator on the other end of the phone.

Broker ignored his conscience about an investment, purposely drove his family off a bridge on the way home.

The winds cry into the ears of the foolish, not listening, hit repeatedly, standing alone.

Whatever direction or position, life is life; from whatever has fallen you are not exempt or prone.

Life is not always rainbows and bliss, volcanos, tornados, and words we want taken out of life's songs.

It is the truth, these tragedies we must face; with YHWH's help, we will have the strength and be strong.

Take heed before our lives are buried and gone.

Endure and always embrace whatever falls upon your soul; repent and answer YHWH's loving knocks.

If you are hit by one or many, know YHWH allows and he blocks.

He holds the invisible batteries to life's clock!

He will sustain you from the different shapes, sizes, and all things that weigh on you; there's

Nothing to be afraid of or shocked by.

He is your loving Father, more powerful than all the falling rocks!

GRAVEL

Did not get that mansion or house on top of the hill and backyard pool.
Prayers and patience often applying the correct rules.
Babies, hard work, promises, stress, not finishing school.
Family, lot of things, and still living in the trailer that was supposed to be a fixer-upper ... a starter?
In the beginning, long hours from the both of us, working harder.
Perfect pair, planning our future, nothing happened in its order.
Dreams were high as mountains we shared, prayed that would someday be.
We based our foundation with love and truth, believing all things are possible.
Our waterfalls were not beyond our reach; we conquered every obstacle.
When the cold seasons had past, we enjoyed hot days at the creek eating melting popsicles.
Country girl, you said I was, walking barefoot on the gravel road.
Together accomplishing all we set out to do, I thank YHWH we did not drop life's unpredictable loads.
Our words kept, we paid back all the ones who helped us out; today's balance zero, nothing owed.
Wind is blowing, and my feet trample the green grass, time spinning, our lives no hidden code.
Sitting on this lonely hill, holding your make-believe hand, did not know our time shared was borrowed.
Feeding the chickens, cows, pigs, ducks, and goats; in between brief moments, go jump into the creek.
Storms and rains, next harvest, rows of plenty, my prayers are sincere, not from pride but from faith I speak!
I smiled through all our seasons of destroyed crops, seemed like a forever unharvest streak.
I smiled because you, my love, your faith in YHWH was strong and never cloudy or weak.
Remember blacktop roads and those bubbles we popped with our feet?

Dirt roads and dust everywhere, picking blackberries in the bushes, we made pies and eat.

Breakfast at night, homemade syrup, biscuits, eggs, that thick old-fashioned bacon.

The smell went through the house, every soul hungry and wakened.

Times we have shared not knowing later, death's shadow happiness would take.

Back down memory lane, losing the twins, Phil and Bill.

Once again broken heart uncovered shield.

I lay in the grass and roll down the hill.

My shoulders, your kisses and love I feel.

You are gone; YHWH has taken my shadow, it does not seem real.

Rows of growth then, now my tears of loneliness are being spilled.

We were not rich; a poor country girl and city boy, together the land we tilled.

Tomorrow could not be put off any longer because Charley the runt we had to kill.

You raised that pig; now he is too big, suffering each day he lives.

We love our animals, that day I saw sadness in your eyes.

I did not see with our seasons of loss you cared for a life that others said, "He is not going to make it.

Look at his size."

Your faith in YHWH concerning a runt, not listening to other's lies.

Charley you nurtured; death was not the answer or question to compromised.

City boy no more; country runs through your caring heart, prayers for a pig, and tender cries.

A country boy repeatedly falls and unquestionable tries.

Being with you a lifetime, hmm, how times flies.

I fell in love with you again; did not think was possible, I was surprised.

I think we spent more time enjoying the land outside.

The world did not exist, our love the trees could not hide.

Horseback riding—one horse two souls—the sun going down, into the night we ride.

That day forward, marriage, we decided.

Coming to that old stable you refused to tear down, Wednesday, I became your bride.

It hurts so much being alone; we were together I thought forever.

Falling in love and doing what's right, city boy-farm life, you were determined,

Smooth and clever.

Leaving me, that thought from my heart never.

My hand, your shoulder, our lives, beautiful waterfalls we made together.

Our home stood through all disastrous weather.

Sitting under our calming tree when life is not smooth like leather.

Our special peaceful place, holding each other, two birds one feather.

Tears, memories, lifetime of us I gather.

Our intimate walks along the trail by the creek, loving me as you do scared you.

Always looking at the paintings the brushes of life drew.

Holding me tightly, teary eyed, heart saying our lives there is nothing I would undo.

What is wrong I asked? Trust in YHWH always; there is nothing you cannot go through.

Smiling. he kissed my forehead, admiring the land and the skies of blue.

I do not know if today, letting go of my hands, he knew.

The harvest, farm, and land, to have him here again I would give away.

Just a true moment with him, no skies of gray.

Sitting on a dying bench, holding hands, praising YHWH for another beautiful rainy day.

Remembering silly things he would do and say.

Acting like children, in the backyard we would play.

The times swimming in the creek nude and then roll in the hay.

Flowers and weeds, he would make me a beautiful bouquet.

Being with him, I believe in marriage; things go wrong, neither one, if truly trying, will stray.

Memories of us not understanding life; he went to sleep last night, and this morning did not wake.

This morning I am alone for real, goes back when we lost our twins, I thought I would break.

His faith in YHWH let me know my heart will not continue to ache.

We shared so many things, our love grew from tiny mistakes.

Remembering that old gas stove, cornbread he tried to bake.

Standing here alone, missing him, these feelings I cannot shake.

I can hear him saying YHWH does not give us more than we can take.

It is the twins' time to share with their dad.

Blessed loving him fifty-seven years, I am thankful and glad.

Crying daily, trying not to get mad.

Remembering …

Two acres of land, imaginations, lots of love, more than some rich folk had.

I am crying because my heart must accept the good things in life attached to the bad.

My heart is filled with issues, questions about a life that was full, now empty and sad.

I wished time; we were blessed to have more.

Life in my womb, YHWH has sealed the door.

Infertility has trapped me in its teeth and jaws.

They are gone, and my life cannot rewind; and I wish all this hurt I could delete

Or gently pause.

Death has penetrated its roots, and my hurting heart is suffocating within its peaceful claws.

Four graves, and we were one family taken just because …

Let love be your daily waterfall, and kindness will be a beautiful door to walk through when you

Walk from this side of life.

No matter what roads or paths you travel.

Judgment of all sins committed He shall unravel.

Back in the earth, covered with rocks, sand, dirt and … gravel.

HEAVEN IS COLORFUL

❦

Grandchildren ask questions that touch your heart and make its inner chambers cry.

A heart filled with I do not know, and eyes wanting to know why.

Questions are on life's pages from birth, remaining after the day you die.

Little minds like sponges, tenderly telling the truth and not letting it get twisted into a lie.

We know deception, confusion, and curiosity is the path the devil wants these little ones to try.

He has a storehouse with wickedness to the world regardless of age, an unlimited supply.

I must pause because I did not know what to say.

Little souls needing to be taught Yah's truth we pray.

So when older, they will know the right way.

So-called goodies the devil tries to use; they will not be tempted or stray.

Prayers around these little ones, from the rising of the sun to its departure at the end of the day.

The Father's holy angels encamp around them where they lay.

My granddaughter came running in my room saddened, tears falling from her little face.

Is it true children of color's souls in heaven won't be placed?

If she were a teenager, it would be simpler to explain, but that is not the case.

I paused again, more questions?

I wish I had long blonde hair and not nappy, and my skin smooth and white.

What's wrong, baby girl? I held her close to me. Grandma, is it true, is it true? What is it? The man on the computer said children of color are going to be with the devil and not Yah because Yah is white.

I kissed her on her darkened skin, saying the man is wrong and not right.

Yah is love; His spirit shines bright.

The man on the computer is living in darkness because he has not the Father's light.

Grandma, will I be in heaven to sing with His angels? Yes, I held her gen
and tight,
Letting her know children all around the world will sit at the Master's feet
and never be judged by the color of their skin. Heaven is not about color
but those who love the Father and let His Spirit grow within.
The man on the computer, we will pray for him that he repents of his sin.
Children of all races will be there.
The color of skin YHWH does not care.
His love for all races, within His Spirit He shares.
Your dark skin and nappy hair are beautiful gifts.
You are a child of the King; let love and kindness be the pages of your
absorbing heart and mind.
Be thankful the Father made you, and you are precious, unique, one of a
kind.
Yah is the Father of many colors; if it were not so, people would be the
same.
Your color or hair texture you do not have to question or explain.
In the heavens is your very own pretty picture frame.
Be proud of your black skin, nappy hair, pretty face, and your Yah-giving
name!
Dying for all races is the reason He came.
Do not let others' hate make you feel less or blamed.
Pray for the foolish, and their remarks Yah will tame!
Do not be sad or afraid; Yah will protect you with His clouds of rain.
Yah made you beautiful, intelligent, not ugly or ashamed.

HIM

✢

Went to this retreat; it was okay. Talked to strangers about things that have attached itself.

Conscience clear as cleaned windows in spring; all is done, and nothing I must fix or tend.

I came alone, unheld hands, no family, and surely no trustworthy friends.

I acknowledged the darkness that tried to hide itself along with my sins.

My mind was like the altered sweet smell of honeysuckles and bitter grapefruit's winds.

I am standing in this beautiful garden of unprejudiced flowers.

The scenery is amazing; when I thought it could not be any more breathtaking, down comes

Yah's peaceful showers.

Awesome with nothing in comparison, its landslide victory over all Eiffel Tower.

Beauty far as my eyes could see, I stand in awe; crisp air I inhale for several hours.

I love this, desiring for this to be penetrated into my life's fraudulent folders.

I glimpse at me back then, tears now, broken dreams, and lies; I am older.

I stand in all this beauty; the façade has fallen, and I'm saddened, afraid, and much colder.

A touch of someone's hand caressing my burdened shoulders.

I looked backwards to see no knight in shining armor, instead a tall, caramel, thin man standing there.

I turned and lay my head on his chest; holding me, he smiled, asked me my name, and in the distance,

Winds singing, "Beware!"

I was indulging in the moment, being weightless of all my troubled cares.

We talked for hours, his moments in life weren't embarrassed, willing to share.

I wanted to remain there; he'd be my Adam and I his Eve.

A life of new beginnings, in my heart I hoped for in the past, experience and believe.

Every encounter with him I buried in my heart's chambers, when loneliness comes, I'll retrieve

This moment, never thinking I deserved or something else to go back and forth between us.

Am I reading a book, its pages, in a trance I follow, I trust,

Watching my unloved real or fantasy die like my life's falling leaves?

With him this moment I didn't care if I was being fed the truth or deceived

This garden, this moment, is what I need.

Why did I come to this retreat?

Am I looking in the mirror, or am I running late, mind racing life incomplete?

This beauty is all I desire, nothing I seek.

He holds me. I've never been held; laughter and smiles are so heavy my heart is weak.

I want some company for all my lonely years of unkissed cheeks.

He holds me tighter, having never been held, only punched and kicked.

I embrace all that he's given my new experience (intimacy) in his masculine, caring arms.

He pins the calla lily and black hollyhock to my cotton dress. "Be not ashamed of your God-given beauty. These

Two flowers can't compare to your midnight beauty or velvety skin."

Look at the black roses' deepest beauty; my love, your heart deserves to hold within.

All these beautiful flowers—different colors, shapes, petals—meaning you, my admirer.

He took me on a journey through time, like an ignited rocket on fire.

I'm on top of the world for the first time, not knowing we've come this high.

Him I want in this garden after I leave here; he's more than an uncontrollable desire.

We were still standing. *Why and how did I get here?* my heart asks. *Have I been dancing with truth*

Or hypnotized by an enchanting liar?

He squeezes my hand, smiles *Let's go* and walks away.

...eart is lonely with no words of encouragement; it cries within the
...ds buried in the earth in the clay.

...want to be in his arms again; if not, this dream or whatever blot out
yesterday.

Wakened by the sun's light, Lord, if this wasn't real, let me go back with
him, I pray.

Find the tomb or place where my Adam lay.

If not, take my breath this day.

My life without him compared to deafen ears, my mouth and heart
combined, no words to say.

If you can't return him, take my breath away!

Wakened by the sun's light, Lord if this wasn't real. let me go back with
him, I pray.

My heart is lonely with no words of encouragement; it cries within the
winds buried in the earth in the clay.

I want to be in his arms again; if not, this dream or whatever blot out
yesterday.

I want him!

If not take my breath this day.

IN HIS PRESENCE

He held my hands, leading me through this beautiful journey.
His beautiful spirit brighter than the stars, His love began to unravel.
I saw many simple things He made—trees, sand, rocks, and different types of gravel.
Sky-blue waters and a mixture of seasons along the path we travel.
He touched my eyes, and I saw the wind.
Turning to the left, seeing all difficulties with Satan with which He had to contend.
Chances given to him; disobedience was limitless and couldn't be mended.
Satan had everything … Why would he commit sin?
I saw this beautiful angel, Satan, and desiring power and jealousy, he welcomed in.
Because of Satan's disobedience, from heaven he was thrown out.
Like us today.
People are people around the world, filled with questions and doubt.
Father, let me stay here with You in the heavens above.
I was surrounded by Him and His unexplainable love.
Can't remember if it was morning, noon, or night.
He let me look beyond, through His eyes to see His glorious light.
He let me see my heartbeat and embrace His spirit that was so bright.
Holding onto Him ever so tight.
His voice was mighty, like the roaring waves on a stormy day.
Being in His presence was a comforting breeze.
The sun's light piercing through the morning trees.
I was afraid and filled with peace.
The gravel and dirt roads we walked upon; He told me to take off the sandals on my feet.
I saw the birthing of fog and its particles within my reach.
Crisp air and melting snow, stretched out sands that surround the beach.
The clouds I touched didn't feel like cotton or wool.
The oceans sang praises to Him, being purified and full.
Winds greeting Him, in their direction they gently pulled.

ade a sweet hickory fire and didn't need wood.

miled at me, and upon my head He placed a warming hood.

e stars thanked Him for His kindness, and the moon danced because

ll He made was good.

He set me at the top of the mountains.

I was thirsty listening to Him; I drank from His holy fountain.

I saw true colors and inhaled nature's peaceful scent.

He let go of my hand; I followed wherever He went.

I saw the scared strolls, the angels surrounding its golden tents.

There were no plans or blueprints.

He placed me at the bottom of the waterfalls.

My hands touched the roots of life and all its glory.

So amazing to see if someday this would be read as a fiction story.

I wanted to see all my heart could take, a blessed day and not be hurried.

I saw the thick darkness of death and evil, and with Him I wasn't frightened or worried.

My eyes beheld the making of man, the day of judgment, life's struggles within.

My heart beat in silence, days of laughter no more; time had come to its end.

He wept for mankind; His Son was the only sacrifice worthy for these lost souls He defended.

His bruises, torture, wounds, hatred from the world, He ascended.

Sorrow and pain were not the plan for mankind He intended.

I felt warmth and love seeing the war and battle that He could only win.

I gave Him thanks, bowing my head and with knees bended.

Valleys of shame, poverty, anger, greed, lies are combined sin.

Not knowing, He was closer than a brother and more passionate than a friend.

Taking me to the northern lights, His words were blankets that filled my heart and kept my body warm.

He showered me with wisdom, knowledge, and understanding; He cradled me in His loving arms.

Destructions' times of sorrows, He placed me in the peaceful eye of the storm.

Netherlands, Africa, Canada, New Zealand, or Japan can't compare to the beauty of being

In His presence.

INVISIBLE FRIENDS

✦

Sitting on a bench talking to an elderly soul, the signs were displayed like an overpriced painting.

He/she got my back; I trust him/her with my life. They have the key to your house and everything else.

We drink, smoke, go to church; that's how it is and what we do. Conscience clear like cleaned windows

In springtime. Like a child believing the myth bats are blind. Present day he/she has taken the

Sparkle from your eyes, waking with him/her, enjoying rays of the sunshine.

Planned a life with him/her, forgetting you were never good at math.

He/she was the sweet melody in your laugh.

Wasn't that your soulmate, better half?

Tears in your heart along with pictures of him/her relaxing in your warm calming bath.

Similarities like a child and their imaginary friend, or believing their abuser loves them.

You were too sweet and too giving; in your home another is living.

All because you let it.

You didn't want to see, years ago, today is the path you were headed,

Foolishly believing the light would scare away the black.

Friendship is what I thought we had.

Handed a mirror, the elderly soul said count them because I have felt the pain

For years, but you remained on its destructive tracks,

Pulling up her shirt of a wounded back.

P.S. Invisible friends—aka jealousy—also desire your jobs, ideas, materialistic things, whatever. Be careful.

JUST PEOPLE

❧

Politicians, false prophets, lawyers, this gigantic worldly franchise.

Majority of people want a slice, their souls they happily demise.

Puppets on Satan's string, money, power, whatever; they're willing to compromise.

Their smooth charm and intellectual speeches of hope for everyone are all lies.

The more they tell and the world follows, the higher their careers rise.

Doctors telling you to take this new drug; it will make you feel better.

Five to ten years from now, in court with these corrupt companies trying to settle.

The side effects they already knew; if not dead, you're on a make-believe journey up the mountains you pedal.

Behind closed doors, these murderers are given an award or special medal.

Traps everywhere—schools, hospitals, day care, nursing homes, grocery stores, churches, our homes, places where we think are safe; it's all a façade.

The ones we look up to have fallen, blasphemed, and chosen to follow wicked gods.

Man and all his riches, knowledge, strengths wants to rebirth Nimrod.

He thinks he's better, more arrogant, smarter.

Years in the making of New World Order.

Wanting it all comes with a price.

Shutting out the good and repeatedly accepting the evil, not thinking twice.

Greedy, sticky fingers and unfilled heart, you roll the dice.

Heart dead, eyes never full, a derailed train that only God can stop.

How many do we know along our way, stepping on others destined to the world's

unjustly top?

The path we choose today at judgment day can't be bargained or swapped.

From the president to the queen, and all others outside and between.

Good or bad, kind or mean?

Rich or poor, tired, dirty, or clean?

Look in the mirror; we are all just people.

LOSING WEIGHT?

❖

Potatoes, gravy, macaroni and cheese, fruit salad, and grilled steak.
Green beans, fried chicken, sweet candied yams, and red velvet cake.
Collard greens, beef rib tips, cornbread, banana pudding piled on my plate.
Food, whatever kind, I love; I don't discriminate.
Standing in a long line, I patiently wait.
My stomach big, butt wide, legs and aching back that hurt.
Gained a few pounds; next week I'll be in the gym, hard at work.
Trying outfits on in the closet—my clothes have shrunk—trying to put on my once-fitting skirt.
Jeans, slacks, blouses, dresses too tight; need more room in my polyester shirt.
Repeated New Year's resolutions; last four, I'm still at the starting line.
Like a kid in a candy store, buffets, weekly specials, soul food, around the clock dinnertime.
Forty-five minutes waiting for a table; I don't mind.
Vietnamese, Chinese, Italian, Greek—foods I enjoy and tastefully eat.
Focusing on dieting, I often cheat.
I'm not prejudiced at all—fish, poultry, vegetables, breads, meat.
Milkshakes, lemon pies, cheesecakes; boy, do I love my sweets.
I've come to terms, side effects, overweight, diabetes, headaches, bloating, hypertension, swollen feet.
Blame it on my parents, heredity, goes back to the beginning's Adam and Eve.
What fruit? Does it matter? Her disobedience caused Adam to be deceived.
My addiction, her decision, my path, overcoming I don't believe.
Thinking I'll be thin or whatever, it won't be achieved.
Sizes are what they are: big, small, medium, extra large, tiny, huge; these truths I eat, I breathe.
I try, but it is what it is, I pray ..., my addiction refused to leave!
One day sitting in church, having overheard gossip about me,
I couldn't believe people, no matter where they are, pretty on the outside, inside dark and ugly.

...king in my mirror, inside I'm okay, but the outer I no longer want to be.

...o my closet of shame and disgust is what I truly am; this I see.

...hands thrown in air, I'll never fit in a size 3.

Beauty was the con that I portrayed and today's truth, tears and razor, time has caught up with me.

My thoughts, questions, so much for thinking church was the answer; my demons they hold the key.

Into a lonely world I didn't belong; the other side I don't know, but from this hurt I'm free.

Sermon after sermon, Bible study, always at the altar for prayer, my addictions God knew.

My demons sat at the table, indulging in foods I'd chew.

I love to eat; when I'd get in my car, crying, this meal I wish I could undo.

Books, magazines, group meetings, it's like I'm in a sinking canoe.

I'm not allowed to hang with the in-crowd because my weight I can't subdue.

I've asked God to help me through.

It seems He's too busy; I'm not worth it so, His helping hands He withdrew.

Dying slowly—I thought it would be quickly—letting go, I realize another smaller me I couldn't pursue.

God, I don't know what to say, wishing I were a caged animal in the zoo.

Blame myself, not my parents, not the world, and certainly not You!

Entangled with thorns and dying branches, buried in self-pity and cemented strife.

Fat kid all my life, no children, family; who'd want me to be his wife?

Next week I'll be sitting at another table, cutting steaks with a knife.

I won't be missed because I was the fat lady sitting in the middle pew.

Hush, My child, I will not let you die.

I am holding you in my bosom, wiping away hurts and pains that made you cry.

I never left you alone; I heard your every prayer, and the many ones you wondered, *Why?*

On the cross for you I hung and died.

Don't you think enough blood has already been shed?

You let go of My hands a long time ago and forgot My scriptures you once read.

Repent, My child, fast and pray.

Take up the cross, and let Me lead the way.

Though you're burdened down, hurt, today you were My lost sheep that went astray.

YHWH talked with me, letting me know I was sinning with the foods I ate.

Understanding comes with wisdom and knowledge, not the wrong carbohydrates.

My food intake still wasn't full, no matter how much was on my plate.

He wiped the tears from my eyes, smiled, and said, ignoring My words caused you to lose weight.

My spiritual food is all you needed; eat that, and watch stress release its grips on your bones.

I'll never leave you; in this life you reap what you've sown.

Daily plant seeds of kindness, hope, truth; in the end, your reward will be love and not disobedience's stones.

When you fall, repent, get up; I'm with you, and in My spirit be strong.

Times of trials and tribulations you will go through, trust in Me, embracing injustices being blown.

Bury My words in your heart; when needed, you'll have like a dog who comes back for his hidden bone.

Trust Me in everything; I'll take away guilt, disgust, unworthiness, all those things that seem strong.

Pray, My child, without ceasing, and one day soon you'll kneel at My throne.

Layers, weights, and all this baggage and it's darkness begone!

Looking at truth, no longer forty-five minutes in line, those buffet tables into the pits I have thrown.

Get up, dust yourself off, you are Mine, not your own.

Gluttonous demons, I rebuke you in Yeshua's name; Get out, you don't belong!

My child, Luke 4:4: "Man shall not live by bread alone.

MIRACLE

I visited the hospital, looking at all these sick, hurting people, not realizing in one of the beds was me. Into the hall's façade, beneath its painted, covered, unseen, labeled "Psychiatric Ward" stands evil, whipping my body with its demonic rod. A glimpse of light he covered from my weary eyes in this prison where I am being mistreated by this wicked guard. My mind and soul were attacked. I closed my eyes and awakened in a cemetery, graves further than my sorrowful, fearful eyes could see. A mirror was handed to me, and the Voice asked, "What do you see?" Pain not wanting to let go of me! The Voice said, "Look around again, and focus on where you are." In my mirrors of hurt, I see hope and life through all the darkness that attacks me. "Look closer, My child, what do you see?" I smiled at Him and said, "A living, breathing miracle."

MOVING ON

———— ⚜ ————

Family photos, letters, and boxed holiday cards.
Planning our future, we gave each other our hearts.
Holding hands, dreaming, nothing could tear us apart.
Saved our pennies and worked hard.
Had babies, always had faith in our Lord.
Asked for patience's hand to lead us throughout life's many complications.
Depended on God to pull us through our difficult situations.
Smiling, watching the kids grow in this unloving world.
We covered them in truth, being protected from hurting hurls.
Thanking the Father for three boys and three girls.
I know we did the best we could in their upbringing.
They had the best education children needed.
Tiny souls, from birth Yah's Word had been planted and seeded.
Standing here today, I feel abandoned and cheated.
The answers I once knew growing like a vine.
Photos once so clear, seems they have faded on the pages of my mind.
Tender moments of just you and I, filling pails with my tears, our well
is dry.
What happened? Vows spoke unity until we die.
Dreams, dreams letting go of balloons, the winds blow like a kite in
the sky.
Weddings, vacations, graduations, was it all a lie?
Sincerity's in our chamber's heart, years today we cry.
Can the materials be mended back together, hands thrown in
the air, backs turned we sigh?
Crossroads, marriage license, dreams, too much, too little, too
late to try.
Questions, sorrows, and confusion ask, Why?
The leaves have reached beyond the heavens; second chances my heart
ponders.
Life, love, laughter, hope; my heart is like the heaven's angry thunder.
The ties have been cut and burned; *By whom?* I wonder.

ems unanswered; the glass was full, now empty, my mind ponders,

er, you said in Matthew 19:6 what God hath joined let no man put
under

Did we not see the signs in our broken home?

Everything is misplaced and scattered.

Marriage, like glass that's been thrown and shattered.

Too many unsaid words and unnurtured love, present day nothing mattered.

Hands held for the last time, pointed fingers who was wrong.

Building a life, making a home,

working overtime repeatedly, the bond is weak, no longer strong.

We kissed each other, putting back boxed cards and letters.

Our marriage is over, and seeds of hope are internally ruined, not better.

Sorry, it's over, nothing to grasp at or settle.

Our marriage is gone, like steam from a kettle.

How can we still love each other when our foundation is gone?

It doesn't matter who was right or wrong.

In each other's arms we no longer belong.

Crying deeply, knowing letting go is the first step to moving on!

MY WORTH

My husband, searching for him I need a map.
My face is to be kissed, not slapped.
Marriage was supposed to be beautiful; I'm caught in this abusive trap.
My back isn't a ladder for you to climb.
Life with you, I'm sinking in quicksand.
My heart isn't for your feet to stand.
My body is tender, delicate, and sensual, not your punching bag.
Lord, give me strength; I don't know how much more I can take.
My mind isn't a code for you to belittle or break.
Help me, Lord, my eyes are swollen, and my soul aches.
I should know where you are and not have to guess.
Faithful I have been, along with its strings of stress.
I'm the blame, you say, because of this hurtful mess.
My unheld hands and tired feet need to be caressed.
You're too busy thinking of her.
My love I give to you only, but you have a sidepiece.
Looking in her mirror, she should want more.
I'm a good wife; you have the nerve to call me an insincere whore.
Love, joy, life, today I open its door.
Finally, being all, I can be through the canal being birthed.
Smiling, acknowledging my value, my worth!

ROTTEN APPLES

❖

In this repeated age cycle, man mentally, physically, and verbally abuses the tender hearts of boys and girls
in every corner of this hurting world.
I stand looking for answers toward the heavens above.
My heart aches because man desires greed and things that don't allow love.
Unanswered prayers, Father, why has darkness in man's heart melted into steel?
I cry for dying people, fading hope, trying to hold onto the many You have sealed.
Into my hurting heart confusion, anger, children taken against their will.
The earth cries for the lives of thousands daily being killed!
Searching for justice in a land where it is blind.
These murderers, predators, laws they hide behind.
Nothing new under the sun, lawyers, doctors, the haves committing the crime.
On this Ferris wheel of a better tomorrow, the sun has lost it rays of shine.
Man has the unknown answers in his so-called lab of perfection.
The news ... Evil feeding the world with its many hypocritical confections,
eating from Satan's hand, sacrificing others to win a predestined election.
We know its victory may seem lengthier, but their season's a quick erection.
Lies, serpents, covering their own asses for protection.
Peace, peace, STDs, the world system is an incurable infection.
The elite, tribulations, thinking they will escape because of their wealthy connections.
Darkness has its hands on the missiles aimed in all direction.
Underground, your new world, bottom of the deep, moon or space.
Tribulation, truth's revelations speak about; if living, all will face.
Nothing new—technology, automobiles, buggy cart, different times, same race.
Satan, disobedient angel, wanted to be Yahweh, thrown from grace.
No matter how old the world is, free will has always been the case.

Good, evil, it began, world formed and void, garden of Eden, the for...
fruit they tasted.

Free will they were given, kicked from the garden to work hard, tilling
land their feet were placed.

Disobedience is like a map a blind man can trace.

Having everything wasn't good enough, obeying Yahweh, they would
rather do wrong.

Why, I asked Yah, didn't He stay in the heavens, His untainted home?

Satan was no longer there, so he didn't belong.

Why let Satan and his angels go on?

Why were You lonely and made man, who You knew was weak and not
strong?

You, all-knowing, knew mankind would never get along.

In this beautiful world, why create when You should have broken his every
bone?

Satan included, like man, wants to overtake Your kingdom, Your throne.

Yeshua was the only worthy vessel to pardon man, giving him free will to
decide his eternal home.

I get no pleasure from the soul that perishes and is lost.

I give all mankind free will; if he allows his faith to be like a wave tossed,
it's on him, I did my part at Calvary's Cross.

Yahweh replied, My child I didn't make rotten apples, not even Satan.

I only made apples.

SEEDS

So many things to do and places to go.
Everything's fast paced, nothing's slow.
Doing things your wrong way, being tossed like waves to and fro.
Doing this and that, several hours you sit at the picture show.
Walks in the parks with the kids, feeding the ducks, working hard to keep your head above the water
Into your garden, waiting for the seeds you planted to grow.
Too many things on your mind; it takes nurturing and love penetrating the things we sow.
Not caring and being patient, doing things expediently, your increase will never overflow.
Breathe, pay attention, listen; taking care of a garden, these things you need to know.
Be obedient and humble, caring for all the seeds you planted row by row.
Life is like a garden; how you care for it will determine rather it lives or dies.
Sometimes you must start all over and try.
Be persistent, gentle, and all the peaceful things from above.
Don't forget to water your seeds with the Father's unconditional love.
The things you're trying to grow are alive.
Whatever it needs, tend to it, and never hold back or deprive.
Whatever your tool, rather it's a mule or tractor with the plow or wheel, take it and drive.
Planting and life are the same; what you put in or not is your choice.
Listen to Yahweh's still voice.
Stop spreading seeds of hate and division.
It grows like a wildfire, in the end more murderous than a train collision.
We can pretend in this life when we stand before Him, our seeds will be proof.
We can't point blame at Yahweh or Satan; the heart holds the truth.
We can't go back in the womb; we can repent and take hold of Yahweh's hand.
Into His scriptures we'll see the falling of Satan and the making of man.

How disobedience caused Adam to till the land.

Follow, acknowledge, take heed, and His commandments y
understand.

Paradise for humans has always been Yahweh's plan.

Eat His words daily, and when you fall, repent; and in judgment His
presence all will stand.

Yeshua was the only worthy sacrifice!

Today, not tomorrow, next week, no time for thinking twice.

The seeds you're planting right now determine whether your name is in
the Book of Life.

SPIDER'S WEB

Was I born with a silver spoon in my mouth or with questions, being penniless, not
having a dime?
Climbing up the mountains of hope, the winds blew me off and on to a breaking vine.
The answers that guided me through this tunnel, my heart is heavy and eyes blind.
The heavens shower me with its volcanic displeasures, seeking shelter and none to find.
In a former life, I do not know if it exists, or whomever I was supposed to be cries within
the pages of my mind.
Whom do I pray to for relieved clouds of uncharitable rains continually being trapped in its time?
Hands of betrayal beat upon my life like I'm the nail.
I stood by the oceans, mind tired and body frail.
Buried in the deep of the earth, covered in addictions, poverty and shame pour from its pail.
I was placed here for whatever reasons, entrapped in this tormented hell.
Birthed into addictions' womb, calming fragrances of relief my nostrils won't smell.
Fingers pointed in every direction, abused child, woman, and man, their stories the winds yell!
No book or movie, its entirety man tells.
Peace, I cried to the heavens, help me, Lord.
Whipped in the womb, alcohol ingested through my cord.
Intersections, stop signs, my life hasn't been easy but complicated and extremely hard.
Fed cocaine through a tube, crack baby was my name.
On judgment day for my trials and misfortunes will my mother be blamed?
Addict at birth, not wanted, discharged from the hospital, no family came.
Thrown in the system and outcast, should have been thrown in the flame.

Had to fend for self, being pushed in the game.
Lies told, things will get better, in the future it'll change.
I'm grown, still that addict, and it's all the same.
From my birth placed in an unwinning fight, I fought.
Not knowing in the spider's web I was already caught!

STOP THE MUSIC

❧

Loneliness, betrayal, happy, mad, free, trapped, lustful, confused, and suicidal sad.

Reading heartfelt cards and smiling, looking at family photos, asking you was this all we ever had?

Several babies along the way, youngsters struggling, not worried, holding each other up, content, and glad.

Two souls becoming one, wanting to be the world's greatest mom and dad.

Moments we framed, getting lost in rainbows of love, drinking its enticing wines.

Standing on the clouds of laughter and joy, his sweet lips kissing mine.

Treasures of rising in his arms, holding on to his words in my heart, between the sheets, and on renewed lines.

Heart beats tears of I'll always be by your side.

In my dreams you are there, awakened by the ocean's waves, its penetrating tides.

Lost in this fascinating tornado, it's a delicious buffet and unexplainable rides.

Intimacy is what we're experiencing, beauty beyond the waterfalls we cry.

His arms holding me tight makes the loser inside me want to try.

We're history, future and present day, building love castles in the sky.

You make me want to live and believe our journey will never die.

How deep is our love, floating on a natural sensual high?

Vows, promises all the same, more precious than silver and all the world's gold.

I'll never betray, bruise, tease; you're my all, and together we'll grow old.

Hold my heart, hold my hand, look in the windows of my soul.

Love is a beautiful gift that people rarely appreciate.

Everyone's cheating, regretting marriage, kids, family, like this was a bad dream and simple mistake.

Our life today is being settled, nothing more to debate.

Once sweet words and showing the world how much you love him/her is now shame, anger, and hate.

Taking her to the movies along with her dad on your third date.

Used to be a puppy on a leash, thinking clearly, forgot about the fat crumbs you once ate.

Young love, throwing kisses and catching, tables turned; present-day dodging bullets and dinner plates.

The flower that grew like a tree is pushed down by the waterfalls of life.

Loving each other, rising with kisses on her face … today divorcing your wife?

Little ones in the middle, crying because Mommy and Daddy cutting their lives with an ugly knife.

It's going to work out; Mommy and Daddy will always love you.

Family and friends trying to put the pieces back together of a broken home.

Dinner is prepared, we got the kids; discuss it, try to make it work.

Let all that anger go. Think about the kids; they are the one's confused and hurt.

Hold each other's hands, it's not too late. Love needs nurturing, try.

Is this over? What about our kids? Do we really want to say goodbye?

The honeymoon is over and trance, we're awake, suitcases packed, hand opening the door.

We knew laughter and joy the clouds would someday no longer pour.

Baby, I'm tired of pretending, staying in this, the love is no more.

Baby, you say I'll always be number one in your heart.

If I'm not with you, I'll be left alone in the dark.

It's going to kill me, picking up pieces, trying to make a new start.

Is there another?

No, he says, you'll be fine; you're smart, beautiful, and strong.

I don't want to be a part of this home.

The love that was like mountains, its roots can never again be regrown.

Baby, not blaming, but where did we go wrong?

Love has withered; I don't know where all these years have gone.

Looking back, no, today in your arms I belong.

No, he says, it's over, no matter what we shared or had.

Tears falling, I'm brokenhearted and sad.

Getting a broom and dustpan, all swept together couldn't have been this bad.

How am I going to get through?

g apart, not knowing what to do.

ow you still care for us … Don't you?

ur love has stood in all kinds of disastrous weather.

What haven't we gone through in our shared lives together?

I don't understand. I love us; you're throwing us away like an unraveling sweater.

I kept ever word, every moment, every card, every letter.

How can you let us go and sort our lives like plucking a bird's feathers?

What's left I must erase or pretend it wasn't, crying pieces of us, crumbs I gather.

Only you I love; my love, you gave us happiness in all our sadness, confused. Was it all a dream?

He says it's over; I don't love you, I don't want us or the kids, that's the truth harsh as it seems.

I want to be by myself, no longer a team.

Ups and downs, we have each other, letting go of me, alone on the dance floor, what does it mean?

THAT HUG

What happened? You were my tears of joy and make-believe
Hope.
My world suns of laughter, your smile loosens the tightening of my heart's chain and
Rope.
When passing by at work, you'd smile and nod.
You saw me and held onto me, seeing through my many façades.
Short time, meaningful words, something to look forward on the job.
When I'd make it home, looking at him, my heart weakened due to hurtful words.
Not wanting to be there anymore; once again trapped with someone my life robbed.
Taking a shower, tears falling, my life a broken record, like the chambers of my heart.
Holding onto you if only in my mind you were standing there.
The end of our shifts we'd talk and enjoy each other, not knowing what the other was
Facing at home's doorsteps.
Desiring a soft moment with you, my heart wept.
Conversations and time with you I enjoy and accept.
Sitting with you in your truck, you holding me, my heart cried because it wouldn't last.
Tomorrow, not knowing what to say; I don't have any plans for us too many times.
Being with others and alone.
With you we're different from what I've seen, hoping happiness is your greeting when
You get home.
Being in your arms for this brief encounter of joy, and my forever pitfalls of wrong.
There is no tunnel, cave, or path to permanent love in the nest that was prepared for my

o belong.

, with you for a moment in your precious arms, I can smile through

he shit I take

om him at home.

Time is all I have with him, and it is an eternity of hurtful words and actions, like a

Beaten rug.

Tears falling again because of you, being captured in the eyes of someone's soul, not

Being used like an electrical plug.

I smile because of your caring heart and

That hug!

THAT KIND OF FAITH

❧

I remember when my faith was at its climbing peak when I was much younger.

I feared no man or beast because I believed in my Father, and my mind didn't doubt or wonder.

His love for me was peaceful; in my disobedience, His anger and chastisement like His roaring thunder.

Accepting Him, my eyes were open wide.

He promised me He'd never leave my side.

I did the same, when things got too complicated, holding on, I lied.

I stopped looking at Him, tried to balance everything myself, and failed, no matter how hard I tried.

I allowed anger and guilt to entertain my soul like a carnival ride.

All that I said and thought I knew I asked myself in my heart, Was it hidden pride?

I didn't understand, remembering when I looked at the heaven's above for the first time, accepting His existence.

How can years later I'm traveling the road of blame and resistance?

I began to smoke weed and drink poisons, allowing Satan into my space, no longer his presence I distance.

I remember looking at a white worm in a puddle.

I began to smile and cry, knowing the Father's love; me in His arms, I am cuddled.

No fear, only faith in Him.

What happened?

I said I'd never leave or betray my Father.

I believed every word that He spoke.

Into my closet of shame and darkness, it's poisons I choke.

Voices in my head, laughter, questions. This journey, was it a cruel joke?

Allowing doubt into my mind, one body became many pieces broken.

Satan flipped me repeatedly, like his God-given token.

Still in denial, Father, why have You forsaken me?

I went to church, fasted, prayed, showed love toward mankind.

et my husband bring me a disease and then beat me for his infidelity.

confused, I questioned, was it me?

urting I couldn't see.

Into my heart You whispered.

Father, bring on whatever. I'll never forsake Thee!

I'm convicted, condemned by my own words. Forgiveness, Father, is my plea.

I know Your love, I'm unworthy.

These chains around my neck, hands, and feet only Yahweh can free!

Back to the little girl in the front yard, talking to the Father, knowing heaven is her destiny.

But the grown-up woman is lost in time on a swing attached to an old oak tree,

Not realizing it isn't too late, believing in the Father to make the oceans stand and earth shake.

Go back to your first love, repent and have that kind of faith.

THE MASTER LIVES

✦

Glaciers, mountains, stars, moon, the heavens above, and all life's beauty between.

Birds chirping, dancing raindrops, creatures drinking from a stream.

Light showers, amazing rainbows, breathtaking waterfalls; what does it mean?

Your eyes, hands, color of skin, the dirt, and Yahweh' breath making the perfect seam.

Your limbs, every molecule within us, God holds us together sufficiently with His invisible beam.

Science tries to figure existence, omitting God, ignoring the truth of James 4:14, life as a vapor.

Buildings, houses, furniture, medicines have parts of trees in them, even gum and toilet paper.

The winds blow, the sun shines, seasons change, and dark clouds pour.

Man studies; the truth is in the scriptures he refuses to accept and oftentimes ignores.

Genesis 1:2, in the beginning the earth was without form and void. Man's curiosity—how the

Heaven's thunder and oceans roar.

He's like the oceans, never full. He may scientifically know the depth, width, and linings of the shores.

Man may know the sacred rituals of the elite, evil deeds on Wall Street.

Connecting my organs and every fiber in mankind, he'll never duplicate its truth, not in this lifetime or

In his dreams or sleep!

Cloning is what it is, artificial making of man; it's in a lab, not by conceptions, and it's not a sheep.

Making of man God formed from the dirt; with His Spirit, Adam was complete.

The Great I Am made man from the top of his head to the sole of his feet!

Yah is more dangerous than a volcano combined with earthquakes, twisters, tornados, and at the same time, e a dove, gentle, humble, and meek.

an searches for answers and asks questions; his mind and heart are
eprobate and bleak.

Worldly knowledge and all its attachments lead to torture and greed's
ugly defeat!

In man's lifetime, he's given a beautiful opportunity with its struggles and
closed doors in My

Scriptures to abide and keep.

Fame, fortune, or the unknown are the things buried in his hardened
heart he seeks.

Wanting to grasp the winds and all its beginnings, he won't have on the
mountain's peak.

God loves mankind and knows his path and ending, placing him in a
world where he can survive,

Not making him His project but giving him his thriving mind.

Man looks at the world angry with God because of many reasons.

If he looks in the window of his soul, he'd be guilty of committing treason!

Wars, poverty, poisonous gases, drugs, crime, and the lists goes on.

The seeds planted in our schools, churches, homes, everywhere have
sprouted and grown.

Mandatory to have permits for things you build on your land; being taxed
due to square footage, it's

the law for the rich and the poor. Who do you think feels the slaps?

The whole world is on TV, the ones watching and the ones being watched;
nothing hidden, it's all a trap.

All the documents are in the government's possession—deeds, wills,
certificates, births and deaths, blueprints, and maps.

Government knows it all—your family visits, shopping, and phones being
tapped.

There are no Democrats, Independents, Republicans; they are on the same
team, sitting on the same misguided lap.

Darkness is within him; all he has accumulated is worthless scrap.

His mind like a radar, claiming things that are not on his life's map.

His knowledge into his bowels of destruction, eating piles of hollow crap.

Man, and all his so-called knowings, will fall in his own predestined trap.

Nothing hidden anymore; darkness has been washed to the sand's surface.

Boiled down to the all-seeing eye the devil uses for his deadly purpo[
We allowed Satan to catch us; he has oiled and marinated us like a du[
Table is set: silverware, chairs, poisonous wine, years of plannin[
mankind's biggest potluck!

Accepting the invitation to the world's biggest party I wouldn't accept.

Matthew 12:40, for as Jonah was three days and three nights in the whale's belly, Yeshua.

Three days and nights in the heart of the earth He slept.

Remember Calvary, the cross, rewind … garden of Gethsemane, where Yeshua wept.

The Great I Am created the heavens and the universe!

I won't accept being second in your life; I must be first!

Stop trying to figure unimportant matters; follow Me and be blessed, or damned and forever cursed!

I'm not dishonest like a lawyer or salesman running a dirty scam.

I am truth and life, all that I Am.

Still not sure? Read My scriptures and teachings. You don't need an X-ray or microscope to examine.

An invitation to repentance and a wedding, the marriage supper of the Lamb!

If you accept, the journey won't be easy; darkness will beat you like a slave.

Don't let go of My hand, be strong and brave.

I am the only One who can save.

I'll never leave you, My Spirit, the Comforter I give.

I'm not dead!

The Master lives!

THERE'S MORE

❧

Pictures in my dreams because my life isn't pretty, and I was birthed into a darkened trap.

Death and sufferings into my aching bones, like punishing sap.

Waterfalls, mountains, the rising of the sun and all its beauty dangle above my heart in its untouchable cap.

A mother having lost everything, unknowingly talks with YHWH with her head on His lap.

My sufferings and pains go further than a topographical map.

Why was I ever created, dropped into this bowl?

Why did YHWH breathe into my body, giving me an enduring soul?

Should have been a fish; then my troubles wouldn't exist, having no arms to hold.

Why is there good and evil in the world both sides want to control?

Why are racism's seeds still growing, and it's century's old?

When the sun is shining, kids must stay inside, not able to take an innocent stroll.

Because of poverty, I must live in a neighborhood where drugs are continually being sold.

Too afraid to go out at night, and the police never patrol.

Last week gunshots; a mother cries watching her child die in her arms.

Where is the love we're supposed to have for our earthly sisters and brothers?

I'm so sick and tired of this; my heart is smothering in sadness for others.

Taking care of our neighbors in the past is like paper that's torn.

My heart is feeble from worries and body worn.

The light shines in, but we're held by death's straps, regretting the day we were born.

On a table my body like a turkey being carved.

Not enough of this or that without love hurting, people starved.

The church, not about lost souls, but how much tithe you bring.

Nothing sacred anymore in the church; it's about social media and how well the choir sings.

To the have-nots hunger, injustice not fit, dying children daily re
sting.
With no morsels of food, help, coincidental happenings into their he
truth ring.
Life being teased daily, they reach, like fish being caught on a string.
The government can't help; it's in debt with its hand in everything.
Every man for himself, can't lean on anyone's shoulder.
Prayed as a child, cupboard empty, hoping things would be better when
I got older.
Crying, there are no brighter days; let me die, I'm tired and sore.
Darkness has taken over; the light shines no more.
YHWH put His fingers through her coarse hair.
For the first time, she felt His presence there.
My child, the crumbs you received, given to your neighbors, you were
willing to share.
All the darkness that surrounds you, you let cracks of kindness break
through.
In your seasons of hopelessness, you did something the rich man
wouldn't do.
In your darkest hours, your clouds of caring were always compassionate
and blue.
Your heart not knowing all your life I carried you.
Your old body has been replaced with a new.
Your mountains of hurt and suffering, besides your fellow man, I pulled
you through.
Let your mortal body change to immortality, and see My everlasting
blessings pour.
Helping your fellow man and putting aside your struggles and needs, in
My eyes, you I adore.
Never putting self above others, always reaching a handout to those
overlooked, dying on life's floor.
Peace has come for you, and all blessings stretching further than combined
shores.
Rest, My child, it's time My kingdom you explore.
When you awaken, you'll be at heaven's door … and
There's more.

THIRD TRIMESTER

❧

All eyes on you, I participated because of your line of work, being an important player.

Meetings and dinners with people from your job, support handcuffed because I care.

Vacationing all over the world, with your parents and siblings sometimes there.

I was your wife and secretary, all reports, documents in our bedroom you shared.

Wanting a family, overworked, stressed, didn't happen out of our reach.

Repeatedly, what's wrong with me into my broken heart you preached.

Different doctors that you knew, making me feel useless and weak.

The problem is me; artificial insemination was the last solution you wanted to seek.

Too much has happened, too many words that can't be taken back.

All my faults you see; what about your mother and her hurtful attacks?

I gave you love; putting up with her shit, that goes further than any train track.

Respect her, that's family; Who am I, the sheep that's black?

I did more for you than anyone, and my face you have the nerve to smack.

Pleasing your family was my deepest desire.

Looking back, I'm mad as hell, and all this shit has ignited my internal fire.

Sorry no more, and this screwed-up marriage, you and all of it, I no longer admire.

Sacrificed me so you could be you; what did I achieve?

Before we said I do, my eyes and heart you purposely deceived.

Thinking you were the sun, moon, stars, and air that I breathe.

You should have erased your e-mail as I have you trapped; you can't leave.

All lies, I'll give you a standing ovation, a performance well played.

I was the unknown dummy, and my sensitivity acts I portrayed.

Thirty-three years, I was your puppet and controlled animal in her cage.

Reading your e-mail, you forgot to delete one last page.

I'm crazy as hell, a woman scorned, I'm on the verge.

I don't want you to touch me; my life you cunningly submerged.

Lies, lies, making me believe with fake doctors something was wr⟨ ⟩ with me.

Thirty years ago, you got a vasectomy!

Gun in my hand, temper has blown, put all your cheating cards on the table.

Thirty-three years, you son of a bitch, my kids you disabled.

The shit those doctors gave me—barren my womb is labeled!

Was all this a sick joke to you? I wanted children; you took that away from me.

I won't give you the satisfactory of probation or penitentiary.

Today, suffering you will endure, and death will not set you free.

I'm going to suck your life from you; thirty-three years you impregnated me with misery.

I loved you through everything, but not this one. *Bang, bang,* a bullet in each knee!

Crying? I don't care. What about my tears, bullshit from your mother you refused to see.

Your queen and all that shit, today, a gun in one hand, an ax in the other; don't see a ram, so I'm going to chop your ass like a tree.

Did everything for you; truth be told, you never loved me.

I'm the weak one, couldn't have children. Look whose begging; I'm the one holding the dam key.

I gave you love; you gave me lies; the world will see you, the real you.

Always wanted to be the center of attention.

Today, what about Ms. Pretty Young Thing you forgot to mention?

Without children, because of you my life was filled with tension.

Your seeds for her placed on hold, a golden pension?

My eggs cut off, but hers gets an extension.

E-mails, e-mails, what to keep, what to delete?

Shot you in the knees, how about a bullet in your feet?

I'm not who you wanted. Who was this man I lie besides and sleep?

I'm "old," "broken down," and "outdated"—your words like raggedy shoes you wore, not wanting to keep.

Ms. PYT, you're committed to clueless, simple, and cheap.

My house I must leave, like trash with a broom you sweep.

are not sorry, you no good, lying, creep!

no do you think you were? I could have poisoned the food you eat.

did you no wrong; you joked about pouring gasoline on me wrapped in a sheet.

Ms. PYT, fresh, and your good wife of thirty-three years put out in the streets.

Sacrificed me for you today, throwing me away, and her you keep?

Undeleted e-mail—I was always bitter and never sweet?

Today all the hell you put me through you reap!

Stop talking, you lying SOB, I'm hurt, mad,

conscience clear, a lioness on the attack!

Let me see how many of your body parts will fill this sack.

Can't have children because of you!

Artificial inseminations, thirty years ago your sperm was frozen.

So Ms. Young Thing, her womb was chosen.

Sorry? No you're not. You're sorry about the undeleted e-mail.

I am beyond feelings, no remorse!

You didn't have to marry me; it was your wicked choice.

I bet today you won't ride out on the same horse.

Jail? I don't care; I'm not afraid of prison.

Have you forgotten that's where I've been thirty-three years? Guess who was the warden.

All my love and sensitivity are like brick, concrete, man-made shit that hardens!

I was a forgiving person, not anymore; your sins won't be pardoned.

Dying? I don't care; thirty-three years with you, I'm already dead.

No, you're too good for a quick bullet in the head.

Years with you, my womb has dilated ten thousand's centimeters, thirty-three years.

Betrayal, hate, lies, abuse, and death.

My life taken and put on this hurtful shelf.

You have choked my soul, there's nothing left.

Look into my eyes, it's time; darkness has taken over, one last push, one last breath.

TO NOT WAKE UP?

❖

Most of my life I have dreamed lots of things—a growing child, my dreams of death, laughter, shame,
and His countless warnings.
Each one my Father spared me, they were real, I felt a taste of hell's flames, nothing flashed
before my eyes; some days judgment came at night and others, quiet mornings.
The little girl who loved the Father, I abandoned her; in my dreams I had grown up, my sins
being judged for not repenting, and looking at this hateful world, I questioned myself, Why bother?
Unable to kick routines in my life that were killing me spiritually, I continued hurting me,
and my pains never ceased, made believe they disappeared; I abused vodka.
Sometimes I repented, staying on a path to destruction, straddled the fence, thinking I was going
somewhere, walking or running in a game of soccer.
This little abused girl in my conscience, always there except she's holding His hands, not afraid,
smiling at Him; she points in another direction to vivid pictures of what happened ... she lets go.
Crying for me, He picks her up and rocks her.
My life and sins, I admit I am the one to blame.
Thankful and glad my Master came.
The spears from Satan, He has the power to block their aim.
Wind, storms, waterfalls, who am I to questioned Him or complain?
I call Him Jesus, Yeshua; He knows my heart, and I know His name.
Remembering at Annie Eastman School, the ground caved in, and hell opened its mouth; I was there with
so many people, I cried, "Forgive me, Lord," and He reached out His hand and spared my soul.

~vakened praising Him because I knew if I died, I wouldn't have gotten
~orgiveness, and the pits of
hell, my due justice, the flames would hold.
Dreams of hell many times; the others I'm in a car accident, looking down
at my dead body, start
running, trying to connect with my hiding soul.
Concentration camps everywhere; I'm in a room, no windows, a handful
of people praising the Father,
soldiers rushing in, beating, cursing because we wouldn't denounce
Yahweh.
It was scary; my faith in Him gave me peace, from Him I refused to turn
away.
Concentration camps hidden in plain sight further than traffic delays near
and far.
Soldiers dressed in black, marching like an army of horses; we were the
souls they targeted
for battle, and it's an unjust war.
I prayed like never, knowing today is tomorrow, and its future the heavens
roar,
bodies beaten, beheaded, starved; look at our scars.
Preachings of old were true, Yah making the earth, moon, sky, and stars.
The doors of tribulations, testing who's on His side, have been opened,
released from its
prison's bars.
Seasons written before the making of man will happen in their correct
time and Yah-given order.
Dreams so many, the peaceful ones, I'm looking at Him without fear of
walking on water.
How can I have so much faith in my unconsciousness trust in the Father?
All my dreams—warnings, I believe—they were and are real; I pray and
hope my faith
before these times will blossom like a beautiful flower.
The end of times is near; His cup of wrath on the living is being poured
right now,
winds blowing, sun still shines, the earth, the clouds, still showers.

Man eating, drinking, disobedience, the misuse of judicial and ma[...]
powers.

Engraved in their evil hearts, the Master has delayed His coming; they are dead men

walking, the coming of Yeshua, no man knoweth the day, second, minute, or hour.

I have seen and done many things in my fifty years here on this tainted earth. I am thankful

His words, seeds, were planted in my soul before my birth.

Defiling my body with men, drinking poisons, eating foods that I shouldn't, killing my

beautiful Yah-given soul, I repent. I am more than all Satan lies of nothing; I am value

set for my Master's worth.

Years of His spirit covering me on my life's journey of disobedience, and I think I can.

Him never letting me go, prayers my mother prayed, growing in her womb, I understand.

I sing praises to the only true King, thanking Him for never letting go of my disobedient hand.

My heart cries from the lining of my soul within, knowing today my Father has a plan.

I repent of everything knowing and not judgment day, life or death before Him I'll stand.

The little girl and her faith have carried me through because Yah made a promise to her.

If she obeys His truths, she'll enter the Promised Land!

I'm worth more than the stars, trees, jewels buried in the earth and the seashores of sand.

The birds, lions, ants, frogs, all creatures, no soul given to them, only disobedient, ungrateful man.

I'm unique—black skin, brown eyes, moles, beautiful smile; He knows on my scalp the exact width,

length, and every strand.

tan's army didn't prevail. I opened the door, dead soldiers everywhere,
anished. White wedding dress trains with white flowers and a green leaf,
then royal blue gowns with flowers of
white, green, and blue.
Angelic choirs sang, "You made it through."
Not looking back anymore, my life, soul, body, mind, Father I give to You.
That dream I awaken this morning, 3-3-2019, repented, and my path to
Him I'm going to do.
Walking, sleeping, dreaming, knowing the truth, my path He guides my
feet.
Through all my life's situations His words my heart continues to keep.
Right path, wrong path, fallen angels, disobedient sheep.
I know my Father has forgiven me.
I know the truth; why should I remain blind and hell's flame reap?
Forgive me, Father, I want to live in Your presence and not die in my sleep!

VANISHING FOOTSTEPS

❖

Thank you, his abuse no more I'll experience as that door finally closes.

Held in your arms, kissing my face, rubbing noses.

Being with you, a brief loving breeze, my damaged weeds turned into beautiful

thistles and blooming roses.

We were closer than a peacock's feather.

Foolishly thinking our love would withstand strong winds and bad weather.

Tears from my abuse into the ocean thrown away; I no longer pounder or into

my hopeless basket gather.

His hard licks, your sweet, tender, kissing lips I'd rather.

Many times we could have been lying next to you, combined hearts, plans of a future together.

With you by my side through all his hurtful shit, I can cope.

I sit on the edge of shredded hope,

crying, reading a Dear John letter.

Life for us, the winds repeatedly cries, "It's not going to get better."

What will people say? Their gossip will roar, and we will never be settled.

Their dirty looks and harsh remarks will hit us like chunks of hateful metal.

Your kisses and heart listened to the hurting woman inside.

You made me want to love for the first time,

making love underneath the moon and watching the sunrise.

Deep within, knowing these precious moments will disappear, like incoming tides.

Looking at me, all my heart sees is love within your smile and starry eyes.

I must get back to my world.

This trance no longer being hypnotized.

Holding on to you, my heart desired understanding truth's path; this isn't wise.

I want to become one with you; when I first laid eyes on you, I couldn't help but flirt.

My heart couldn't be still while my curious mind undressed, buttons falling from
your shirt.

Making love to me, his bruises and hits no longer hurt.

You found the knob my body needed, unlocking it's hidden door.

Caressing me, I was taken to happiness, from its sensual mouth juices pour.

When I thought, *That's it,* kissing my feet, squeezing my thighs, a completely new level.

All that shit he pounded in my heart, that very moment you took away with
your loving and caring shovel.

I never knew love like this before. I was afraid being with you, the angry clouds would shut its doors.

When I came to myself, you were inside my heart. Him—the abuser—I didn't
want anymore.

Talking on the phone, I could feel your sweet voice dripping on my pulsating
breast like honey.

I wanted to be in your world and enjoy things in my life that shouldn't be.

I've fallen in love with a man whose fruits are always bittersweet.

A man who loves me and will not walk up on me with his angry, hateful, stomping feet!

A man who made unforgettable love under cotton sheets.

So good when we're apart, I experience complete ecstasy.

Loving you in my mind or not, real or fantasy.

Brief encounters, opening my teary eyes of joy, body trembling, heart racing, and you're lying next to me.

Am I losing my mind?

Exploding volcano, now free.

This rage, this love, this—I don't know—can no longer be hidden, chained, or kept.

You came into my heart loving me; you say you're sorry but came only to help.

Thank you again for opening my eyes to freedom. In an instant you're leaving me.

My heart wept.

Remembering this loving man, who I lay besides happy and slept.

You're leaving me with unexplained concepts.

All rituals and repeated sermons I was prepped.

Today crying, trying to find your

vanishing footsteps.

WATERFALLS OF A MOTHER'S HATE

❖

There are no tears remaining in the chambers of my unforgiving heart.
I'm awake, and of this nightmare I no longer want to be a part.
Sitting here being dissected, not having the answers when it first started.
Her love toward me has always been distorted.
I remember when I was ten years old, I had the flu, and my presence she avoided.
Child alone often, Mother's in the room, sad memories recorded.
I carried unbearable loads, like a mule hitched to a cart.
Nothing was good enough; having reached every finish line, I was still short.
I wanted her to love me. She wasn't willing, not even to pretend to play the part.
Countless prayers, seeds of love for me, God plant in my mother's heart.
I joined every sport's team and club.
I didn't make it because no one wanted to stand by me, the fat girl, don't touch, don't rub.
I was given a team jacket; my job, the showers and pools I scrubbed.
Lying to her, I made the team, her arms my heart she refused to hug.
If only she knew the things I did for a sprinkle of her love,
letting these nobodies walk on me like a rug.
Their hurting jokes and name-calling poured daily from its hateful jug.
Would it better if I ran away or was no more? In my heart, I wrestle and tug.
Every test and all exams I brought to her stamped "Awesome" and labeled.
"I'll look at it later," then put it on the countertop or table.
Some days I thought loving me she was unable.
I thought she was lonely; I prayed for God to send her a spouse.
Before her birthday, I'd mowed the lawn and painted the house,
went to the mall and bought her a beautiful blouse.
"No, thank you," came from her.
Same response if I had the money for diamonds and furs.
Instead, that's my job to take care of the house and yard.

Bended knees, put love in my mother's heart, dear Lord.

Thinking if I looked a pinch like her, I wouldn't ever be teased.

I thought beautiful things of her and tried to show her, accepting the truth she wasn't pleased.

Always in prayer, fasting for her love on my bended knees.

God didn't answer; at night my forehead she didn't kiss, or my hands squeeze.

Continually asked God in my mother's eyes for me, but is darkness what she sees?

Not even, "God bless you," when I purposely sneezed.

If I had one loving picture in my heart of her toward me, I'd internally freeze.

Lies in my past of her and I lying on a hammock, listening to the birds in the trees.

Feeding the ducks in the park, sitting on a bench.

Truth be told, the winds of love from her to me, hands of time has quenched.

Wishing one day God would bless me to fix her heart with His loving wrench.

Multiple prayers, heaven has shut its doors.

Love from her to me, the clouds will never pour.

My birth till now, Mother hasn't shown love; today I'm forty-four.

Fat girl in the corner, the world continues to pass by.

Love from her, again it's impossible, no matter how hard I try.

Within my heart, going back to my childhood, having a loving mother, I lie.

God, I'm sixty-seven years old; the hurt remains, and my heart wants to cry.

Twenty-three years ago, this unloving woman You let die.

Confusion runs through my heart, along with questions, I sigh.

I'm angry, with You, God, knowing and not knowing why.

You couldn't make her love me; what's left?

Her last request, book of truths put upon her heart; she was a book of uncaring lies.

Her truths she left for my eyes.

I'm okay with the writings; its contents I'm not surprised.

Not sure of entering the peaceful afterlife, think this would piece
the broken fences, making it better?
My unloving mother tries to explain a lifetime in a five-page letter,
like purchasing the wrong color sweater.
Meaningless words between the lines; it's too late.
I doubt if her feet will walk through heaven's pearly gates!
These unspoken words supposed to be her good deed, so hell's fire she'll
escape.
I prayed, fasted, still the fat ugly kid, coming home from school, handed
the same plate.
My birth mother always making me feel useless, small, never worth
something or great.
Darkness, shame, disgust are some of my daily truths you'd illustrate.
Laughter, kindness, a tender smile from you to me you refused to
demonstrate.
Continual prayers so my mother wouldn't treat me like a loveless child.
God, turn her frown for me into a loving smile.
I guess loving me hate and anger pushed it from its pile.
Thinking if I go to the bottom of the pool, things would change.
They didn't, no matter how hard I'd swim.
Dying, she knew her eyes growing dark and dim.
In a letter, with her dried tears saying I look just like him.
Looking at me like I'm a disgusting rag or dirty film.
Never knew if his name was Johnathon, Jason, or Jim.
Lied to all my life, he died before I was born.
Maybe that's when my petals of a loveless child were formed.
Through her eyes I'll never be my mother's precious charm.
I needed her blankets of kindness to keep me warm.
Instead, her words were deadlier than a yellow jackets' swarm!
Every other month I visit her well-taken-of grave.
I wish I were free from my childhood and its unlovable cave.
No tears, no matter how the winds and trees wave.
I love her still.
My mother's gone, standing here reading lies on her tombstone.
Loving mother, tender and sweet, peaceful house she made a home.
Another visit I stand or sit talking to my mother for two hours.

All cried out for you, Mother; each spring I leave a bouquet of flowers.
Wherever you are, I pray joy in your tormented soul the clouds shower.
Questions asked,
God, why didn't You let me die where I lay?
Mother dear, why didn't you leave me in a field, bag over my head, suffocating in a bale of hay?
God, please make Mother love me I pray.
Why so many harsh words to a child, a mother would say?
Broken pieces, that's me again; God, twenty-seven27 years ago, my mother You let die.
All the bad she did, my tears are like a well gone dry.
I'm confused, I'm grown, I still love her, wondering why.
Nothing I did was good enough, no matter how hard I'd try.
Your walls of torment you built; I pray God has replaced with brighter drapes.
This darkness you rained on me daily, its layers I continue to scrape.
I ask one repeated question: Why didn't you give me away?
I pray in God's garden if forgiven, your mouth will taste His loving grapes.
I wish you would have told me I was a child of rape.
Thinking about the afterlife, she leaves a five-page letter.
Hoping her odds entering heaven will be better!
All truth, all lies, will her soul enter heaven's gate?
This five-page letter doesn't mend the broken pieces of a lifelong fence, making it straight.
Her words, truth or lies, it's too late.
Forty-four years, her darkness the chambers of my dying heart ate.
Maybe, just maybe, today my childhood and adult life your tortures I'll escape.
I know you were raped.
Mother, daily no hidden secrets, I knew I was a mistake.
Looking at me, shame and anger were the foods you put on my plate.
I did everything for you knowing I was an unwanted weight.
Truth be told, my preordained fate.
Years believing, today years confirmed I was drowning in
waterfalls of a mother's hate.

WHAT'S LOVE?

———— ❧ ————

A mother working two jobs, trying to feed her four kids and keep the leaking
roof over their heads.
An eleven-year-old boy, caught selling drugs, behind bars because of situations,
crying, confused, and scared.
The preacher who stands in front of lost souls speaking Yah's Word, truth in the
scriptures he doesn't apply to himself, addicted to unprescribed meds.
An abused girl stands under the streetlight; her pimp takes his, leaving
her wandering in the gutter with no decent place to lay her throbbing head.
The peaceful wife, knowing her husband's infidelities, keeps her silent mountains of
hurt, tears, and pains lying next to him in bed.
The good doctor who's concerned about his patients, in the closet burns himself
because of hurtful words his abusive father said.
Boy in junior high school falls in love with his teacher, told she's not leaving
her husband.
Last week the boy jumped off the roof;, this morning he is brain dead.
Drug dealer foolishly believes good will come from what he's doing in the long
run.
Initiation to belong, boy drives through a park where kids playing, he
fires—ten children, eight dead
two in comas—because of unnecessary bullets from a gun.
People in a cult looking for something, foolishly being led by Satan's minion,
bowing now to the moon and worshipping the sun.
Mother and father considered good people. Their daughter just died, and they couldn't
understand.

Angry with God, jump off a cliff, holding each other's hand.

Lawyer who made it to the top doing unimaginable evil, having it all today, mindfully sticks his neck into life's predestined blades … death's fan.

Having overcome everything by all means necessary, you reap what you sow,

your baby, good or bad, no matter how high on the mountain you stand.

In the beginning, doing the right thing was your temporarily plan.

He's my husband; when he beats me, it's not him. We love each other, but the world

makes him feel like he's not a man.

Satan, I'll give you things—money, wealth, power—whatsoever you desire.

Eyes wide open and blinded by greed, knowing he's a liar.

Woman high on cocaine sets her children on fire.

People searching for a quick fix in life.

Starring at the rainbow, unknowingly cut their wrists with a knife.

If I do better, he won't cheat or hit me; I'll google how to be a good wife.

Don't be the boy who cried wolf or the hurting little girl in the bottle on the corner of the shelf.

People wanting to love and be loved, others not caring only to think of self.

Be still, listen, and take a deep breath.

What's love? John 3:16: For God so loved the world that He gave His only begotten

Son that whoever believes in Him should not perish but have eternal life!

WHICH WAY?

❧

A little girl looks at her siblings sitting under a tree, eating cake and ice cream.

The sun is bright as the stars, a lot bigger; when finished around the tree, playing and laughing, they scream.

Mom stands in the back door, tears in her eyes, not knowing if she's looking at us or in a daydream.

Our lives, I wonder if possible, she'd write a different theme.

I wish Daddy would love us; instead, he treats her mean.

In the kitchen hard at work, cornbread, yams, and our favorite mustard greens.

She puts love in every meal, especially her fried chicken and red beans.

I believe her greatest joy is sitting at the table, looking at the smiles on our happy faces.

We have lived in many places.

Love has been the picture her heart has repeatedly shown.

Laughter for her soul, another direction the winds of time have blown.

I blamed her for us being removed from our home.

Separated we were into a life of plenty; things are the words to a new song.

The sun, moon, and stars continue in the heavens, pushes time further on.

I have more, I'm happy, I prayed Mom was all right; God, if we're not returned, make Momma strong.

The people we lived with had more things to give us; in time I realized here I don't belong.

When we'd meet at CiCi's Pizza or Zemurray Park,

Mom would hug us so tight, I wondered if God held her alone in the dark.

We played, running around, so much love Mom could work for Hallmark.

Her life of few joys and much pain, her tears would be her trademark.

She looked at the ducks in the pond, and people's dogs bark.

Faith was held in her heart, knowing in the future on the path together we'd embark.

Smile on her face while we enjoyed a meal at home.

My twin, Donna, and I were together; our older brother, Joel, was with his dad, Mr. Joel; my oldest sister, April, and brother Abraham were together; Lillie and Samuel were together; and Stacey was alone.

It's eight children; seven of us have the same dad, but the oldest brother a different dad.

Not having much with Mom, petals of love is all she had.

I knew she loves us; in life you take the good and work through the bad.

When our visit ended, through her false smile I knew she was deeply sad.

We would have come home sooner, but her family didn't want us, not shown on her face,

within she was confused, hurting, and mad.

I guess God gave her a chance to have a little time for herself.

Having eight children—five boys and three girls—prayers, hoping we returned, she often held her breath.

If not, a bottle of pills would be her untimely death.

God was always there to pull us through.

Joel was with his dad; Stacey was alone, her heart covered in darkened blue.

Joel was gone nine years, and for us, two.

Mom continually prayed that someday we'd all be together; God allowed it in its seasons due.

Her childhood I wouldn't want to put on either shoe.

The beauty of our separation and reunion God already knew.

The Lord's Prayer and scriptures she penetrated within our tiny souls.

Book of Truths—the Bible—regardless of your ages, the heavens unfolded.

Be whatever you desire, knowing God's arms aren't too short to hold.

Make sure He's included in every goal.

Life has beaten Mom with its cruel spikes and lengthy pole.

Darkness and hurt, with endurance from the Father, poured into her overflowing bowl.

She's one person, two parents; if I had a choice for others, they wouldn't have a chance, young or old!

I see things differently; she tried her best to make our house a home.

A new trailer we lived in momentarily, then later, she sat at the table, eating alone.

Pictures on the wall, Aunt Kal next door, our foster parents seldom let us call Mom on the phone.

Stacey called Mom more; the things she endured there with them into Mom's heart, sadness opened its door.

Foster parents for my oldest sister, repeated itself, the clouds pour.

Mom wasn't right, no matter what the foster parents did,

because of her lack of guidance, the state took her kids.

Mom did all she could, meetings after meeting and classes weren't enough.

She prayed in our hurting heart, and God made the weights from others not so thick and tough.

Mom prayed seeing fresh marks and bruises, lies told, boys are rough.

A lifetime of His words planted and seeded.

Thankful for God's Word yesterday, tomorrow, and today desperately still needed!

Mother, thank you for your prayers for the eight of us and twelve grandchildren, number thirteen on the way.

No matter what happened, your prayers, we weren't cheated.

We know and have His words to shield us from life's darts.

We know falling in life happens, but with all our misplaced pieces, God can mend every part!

I forever thank God for His words you engraved in our hearts.

In my prayers for you, Mother, I pray.

I look back and smile; you couldn't get us things, so at Walmart you'd put them on layaway.

It wasn't so much things we didn't have, I now know; you gave us love through our many skies of gray.

Looking at things, it wasn't we didn't have a car or fancy furniture; you gave us a clean place for our heads to lay.

Pillow to pole things, love you gave; we never thirsted or lacked.

All situations being here and there, my mom standing in the door, looking at us eating cake and ice cream in the back.

It didn't matter if we were in a new trailer or one-room shack.

Boys in the back, girls on the floor playing jacks.

Tears from your heart to ours, thanking God He held the tracks.

Mom, I sometimes feel like you, the sheep that's hurting and labeled black.

You say when you look at me you see the young you; it's sad.

Through all the stones and brick walls, Mom, you really are my mom and dad.

I know I do things that make you worry and not understand.

Through it all, I know, Mom, no matter what, I have your heart and helping hand.

I know you only want what's best for me, a hardworking, nonabusive, good man.

I know these same waters; your feet have walked through its endless sands.

The barriers will fall because in the heavens, for my children and me, God has a plan.

Repeated prayers will someday bless me and my children to enjoy a solid piece of needed land.

When that day comes, I pray, Mom, you'll reach out and grab my hand.

Until then, Mom, I must do this: Remember the woman being pushed to the wall

because you repeatedly stood in front of life's unhealthy blades of its fan.

My blinded eyes, I don't know the end of this unloving span.

Like you, Mom, in time I won't continue being somebody's bedpan.

Remember the battered woman named Ann?

— -Seanna Lackey

YAHWEH, IT'S ABOUT YOU

❖

I got so caught up in my book, the gift Yah gave me, and forgot about the gift-giver, my Father.

I am sorry, I'm so sorry, Father, You have given me words; I have been selfish and

not appreciative. I thank You for the very breath I breathe, I thank You for my family, and

I love You. I thank You for allowing me to see You and ask for forgiveness. I'm sorry.

I need You; I lift my hands to You. You are love! You never ever left my disobedient self.

I don't understand, but I am thankful. Heal my family, neighbors, friends, enemies. Put Your

love in me; if I should fall, whip me with Your righteousness please. I can't afford looking

back; I don't want to be lost. I need You, Father. Whatever my past abused childhood, now

I leave to focus on Your umbrella of love that has been my shield. I truly forgive every hurting

soul who abused me. My hands I lift to You. Wrap me in Your merciful bosom and undying

love. Put Your love in me for all life. Let me love everything You made because it all has

a purpose, from mankind to the smallest grain of dirt. Shower me with Your peace to withstand

every wind, storm, and my dirt piles that seem like gigantic mountains. Heal my husband internally

and his flesh, renewing bruised organs. I want us to live, and we give You praises. My daughters I want You to show them

they can with You.

April, clothed her in confidence and trusting in You, grip her inner soul. Just because her wings are clipped doesn't mean the Father can't repair His hurting angel. In the present, let her know

she's smiles of joy and no one's rug or punching bag. Let her precious feet feel your tender clouds.

Pour oils of her unknown beauty, and she's like a field of Yah's roses filled with His love.

Lillie, rekindle her faith that's big as the moon, if only she remembers. Life has covered with its rays

things that won't last. Be the voice of hope to others who have fallen into the same pair of

hurt-fitting shoes. Step into Yah's preordained path, my child.

Stacey, I pray, Yeshua forever be the root of her, His growing tree, and not let the winds push her into amnesia,

forgetting who gave her true beauty, His Spirit, His words that go further than the oceans combined.

Serving Him who's the way, truth, just, and forever kind.

Seanna—my baby girl, twin number 1—I know and understand your hurt because your path I have been

traveling for years. The Father's grace has put me on an eternal path to Him. Pray to Him the

hurt won't last. He will strengthen you to be the angel you were born to be.

Donna—my precious baby girl number 2—I love you and realize your deafness isn't your weakness but your

strength. I hope Yahweh continues to protect and use you to be the tool that one day won't need fixing,

being able to help others. I love you so much, even though you don't believe me.

Joel, I cry so much for you because we were separated nine years. I love you so much and know the

Father has plans for His son. Your heart has a library of unread books the world will be blessed

to read. Yah's Word has been planted in the chambers of your heart while growing in my womb.

His path you must walk freely upon. You have so much of His love inside you. Letting go of things in this life, my son, and holding onto Yahweh's hand, only then you will begin to live.

Abraham, my darling son, it seems laughter was given to others. Not so, my son. Yahweh has clouds

of joy awaiting you. Don't get lost in the things that are trying to take your faith. Trust only in Yah!

Through your heart's tears, on the other side is eternal love with the Father. Hold on, and whatever

Satan tries to block or darkens, look to Yah, and see all that He has for you. Samuel, my Samuel, dark clouds and rain fill your heart with, "I'm tired, Momma." Don't give up, my son.

Yahweh is not done with you. The thicker and darker the clouds, the blessings are more abundantly

on the other side of all your disappointments and pains. I gave you to the Father, never leaving you alone.

That path to Him you will soon walk upon.

My children, the only thing I gave you of value was and is Yahweh's Word. I proudly say that because

I prayed more with you all growing in my womb and being small. It's a shame I let go of His hand

and temporarily lost hope and custody—two years without you all and nine without Joel. My prayers to the

Father were stronger and deeply sincere. I love each of you and prayed you return to your first love,

Yeshua. No matter what situations come your way,

Yah loves you and there can be peace in everything if y'all let Him. I am sorry for so many wrong things.

Please forgive me and know I love you all. I apologize to the Father for thinking I was ugly

and not worthy of love, having forgotten the Father. I look back at my beautiful babies and

realize if I were so ugly, how could these beautiful babies have my features? I stopped listening

to the dark voices and let His light shine through that never left my unworthy soul. I love y'all.

I know now it wasn't about Lillie; it was about You, Yahweh!

YAHWEH, IT'S IN YOUR HANDS

❖

It's Wednesday, and group meeting is full for the first time this afternoon.
I'm so angry I'm in this thing on wheels. I can move my fingers but can't feed

myself with a spoon.
I'm hooked on meth. I keep abusing it. In the mirror, my life is like unsewn straws

falling from a damaged broom.
I was raped; by who it doesn't matter. I was a virgin, got HIV. I know my petals

to a beautiful future will never bloom.
Twice a week here for a year. This is it. The man gets up, kicks the door open, and

leaves the room.
My family was cursed with drug addictions; today I accept it couldn't be clearer.
I prayed. God refused to deliver me. Three years ago, car accident, I can't walk. I see

the culprit daily, looking in my mirror.
My mom traded me to get high.
The things they did to me. Present-day several times I cut my wrist, overdosed on

pills, wanting to die.
I'm mad, angry. God, why did You let them do this to me?
I can't have children. This medicine I'm taking, I'm confused; my mind is somewhere,

and darkness is what I see.
You counselors, therapists, doctors, say look within breath, find yourself.
Dammit, I love my wife. Everything was good—house, job, kids, Seven months ago

she just left.
A little boy enters the room. I can't see. My health is daily struggles rather preordained,

or not living is my jury duty.

I'm eight years old, have cancer, diabetes, failing lungs, cystic fibrosis, tumor on my brain.

Blind, but I still see God's beauty.

I know I'm dying; I'm not blaming heredity, the unknown, or anything because I know

for me God has a plan.

Look around this room with your seeing eyes. You're here no matter what abuses—verbal, physical—

mental problems or addictions you have. You're alive! Faith, hope through all situations

is the cure for us to continue to stand!

I know for a fact when I close my blind eyes, seeing or not, I'll be with my Father

in the Promised Land.

Because

Yahweh, it's in Your Hands!

YAHWEH'S GARDEN

⚜

Breathe in and exhale, thanking Yahweh in His garden; I escaped the ending with brimstones
and the flames of eternity's hell.
In this beautiful garden, His children and angels aren't the third of heaven who due to disobedience
have fallen.
This new heaven and earth, no Satan, no darkness, only the Father and His Light
dwell!
The chambers of my inner being, unexplainable love, joy, laughter,
infinity's tenderness my eyes and feet compel.
He places me at the mountain's top, His beautiful breath strengthens me; I'm no longer frail.
I stumble, He picks me up, and in His warming bosom I am held.
My tears of thankfulness leave a remarkable, undeniable trail.
Look around and see all Yah's beauty, His Spirit; the flowers, creatures, and earth give
Him praises, untainted beings, lions, elephants, and gazelles.
There are so many creatures, all loving the Father; petals, furs, leather above, beneath,
on land and hidden within its shell.
His extraordinary love for life, calming fragrances rosemary, frankincense, and eucalyptus I smell.
His beauty and love into all ears the petals tell.
He smiles and hands me soothing Yah-made oils in His overflowing bottomless pail.
Heaven on earth, finally drinking from my Father's never-evaporating well!
True beauty beyond the waterfalls of life. His Spirit so amazing.
I stand, trying to grasp all this, and to Him my thankfulness, my mind gazes.
I know this is real.

He went away to prepare a place for His obedient ones in this garden—no moon, stars, or

sun, just His Spirit shining brighter than all life's blazes.

The garden is filled with many tender thorns, tulips, roses, wisterias, and rows of daises.

The animals and all life forms, petals, wings, hooves, hands, eyes, horns, etc., give Him praises!

This garden is not only beautiful, the fruits so memorizing He lets us taste.

I know within my spirit this is an anointing, a peaceful place.

He walks with me and holds my hand; I'm crying because unconditional love is

what I see when I look at His face.

If I were to get lost in this beautiful maze, I'd be okay because His love isn't hard to trace.

He put everything in its proper order and place.

He fills me with love, so much my tears won't stop falling.

I thank Him because in that other world, often I ignored His merciful calling.

I love Him more than eternity!

I love Him holding my hand; I'm here with Him because I'm free!

There is no love like His; I can feel it as well as the animals, earth, and His clear seas.

We all give Him thanks, the ants, whales, spiders, and bumblebees.

I look at this beautiful scenery; nothing is more beautiful than Him.

I can swing from the trees and in unpolluted waters swim.

The air is pure, His Spirit is forever. Bowing before Him, roots, branches, limbs.

No chemicals being sprayed, covering my eyes with blinding film.

This garden, no sickness, no man-made diseases, no poisonous foods, no cancer!

I love Him so much; technology, the internet, encyclopedia, or dictionary aren't needed here. He is the answer.

I feel His Spirit when He lets go of my hand.

I wandered through this amazing garden, trying to understand

why He loves me so. I'm sorrowfully crying. He says, "I'm nothing like man. In this garden, new heaven and earth, you are like Me. Don't you know before Adam and all the others, My garden and kingdom have always been My plan

for longsuffering, faithful, enduring man?

The earth and everything were to help life. Today you're standing where milk and honey

continually flow. This is your Promised Land!

Come with me. Put your arms around the lion and the bear; next to the flamingo you stand.

Let's walk upon the waters and look beyond, and count the grains of sand.

Listen to the birds sing praises to Me.

Turn around. The waterfalls I created, this garden, your destiny.

No need to take your sandals off; My Spirit dwells in you, this special place,

My sanctuary.

My truths in your spirit you will eternally carry.

Freedom, peace, love, and no darkness have been what this is all about.

Be still, and listen to the mysteries that the winds shout.

This is life, My light that shall never go out.

In this new heaven and earth, there's no vacancy for doubt."

1 John 3:2: Beloved, now are we the sons of Yah, and it doth not yet appear what we shall be but we know that when He shall appear, we shall be like Him for we shall see Him as He is.

MOTHER

I love you and want you to know, you're my everything. I'm so happy to be your daughter

And grateful, to have been born into you. You are the greatest mother a child could have been given.

I'll love you forever, you've given me so much knowledge and wisdom. You mean more to me than you will ever know.

I pray you find peace and happiness, your smile and happiness have always been what pushes me to do better, be better, and succeed. I, only hope I have made you proud. There is no other being on this planet with a heart and spirit, such as yours. You are the trunk to my tree of existence. YAHUSHUA the roots and YAHWEH the planter. I will continue to grow and flourish, because you have watered me well, and surrounded me with YAH'S LIGHT.

Printed in the United States
By Bookmasters